Basic Psychic Hygiene

A Handbook of Exercises and Common Sense

Sophie Reicher

Basic Psychic Hygiene

A Handbook of Exercises and Common Sense

Sophie Reicher

Ellhorn Press
Hubbardston, Massachusetts

Ellhorn Press
12 Simond Hill Road
Hubbardston, MA 01452

Basic Psychic Hygiene: A Handbook of Exercises and Common Sense
© 2008 Sophie Reicher
ISBN 978-0-6152-2425-1

Printed in cooperation with
Lulu Enterprises, Inc.
860 Aviation Parkway, Suite 300
Morrisville, NC 27560

To my students past, present and future.
To my teachers past, present and future.

May this book be one more link in the chain.

Acknowledgements

Many thanks to my wonderful editors at Ellhorn Press, to Dagian for proof-reading the early drafts of this manuscript, and to K. C. Hulsman for designing the cover. This book could not have come into being without your hard work. Any errors contained within this text are purely my own.

Contents

Introduction

Training psychic gifts has been part and parcel of my life for nearly twenty years. It began from the sheer need to find a way to survive, and moved to the need to understand what was happening to me as my own very strong gift of empathy developed. Long before I ever practiced magic or any form of occultism, I used that particular talent. I didn't have a choice—I was born with it, and it only got stronger as I grew. Those born with the proclivity to develop psychic talents find the world a far different place from those who are "head-blind" or "psi-null". To an empath, for instance, the world is a battle ground of conflicting emotions, all of which pummel those wired with the ability to experience them directly with the force of physical blows. To the telepath, it is a jarring, loud morass of noise that never stops; to the seer, a confusing whir of color and images, people and experiences to which the average person is blind. Learning how to manage, control and thrive is more than simply the indulgence of an overly besotted New-Ager; rather it's a matter of pure survival.

I am thoroughly convinced, after nearly two decades of teaching students to utilize and control their psi-talents, that a sizeable percentage of people on psychiatric medications or in mental-health facilities would instead benefit from this type of training. I long ago lost count of the students who came to me wanting to know if they were going crazy. Some had tried going to a therapist or psychiatrist for help, only to find that the help provided did no good at all, whereas learning to actively use and control their gifts did. Nearly all had been diagnosed with clinical depression and all of them suffered high levels of anxiety and stress. Now this is not to say that every single person under a psychiatrist's care is really psychic! Nothing could be further from the truth. I am simply saying that strong, untrained gifts can cause a person to doubt his or her own sanity. When they do seek out help from the mental health profession, unless they are very, very fortunate, this profession is unprepared to credit their experiences with any degree of truth and is therefore unable to provide effective help.

We simply don't live in a culture that understands these things. It is something outré, arcane, fanciful, and even dangerous.

Unfortunately, it is not often fanciful to those who actually *possess* these talents. Whereas most people experience the world through a sensorium comprised solely of sight and sound, smell and taste and touch, those with mind-gifts have the pressure of at least one added facet to contend with, and that added facet can make the world a confusing and sometimes unbearable place. Properly controlled, these talents can be immensely valuable to the individual him or herself and, in some cases, to their communities. They have the potential to enhance one's life if and only if they're trained. Sadly, such training can be very difficult to find even in occult communities. I was fortunate; I stumbled upon a series of novels that dealt fairly accurately with the gifts and some occult literature from the early 20th century that also offered solid, practical suggestions for basic training exercises—works like those of Dion Fortune, Denning and Phillips, Israel Regardie (for those of a more ceremonial bent than I). When I first became Pagan in the early 90's (which also coincided with my beginning the practice of magic) these authors were still occasionally being discussed. Within a decade, however, they had fallen almost completely out of favor. It is surprising today to find newcomers to the Pagan community (and even worse, to the occult community), who have even heard of Fortune, let alone read her work. To make matters even worse, if such a thing is possible, the current literature out there on anything approaching psychic self defense all too often provides inaccurate and even dangerous information (white light, ladies and gentlemen, is not a cure-all).

There have been some very good and useful books published in the last decade, despite my own rather grim account of the state of the community. I provide a list of suggested reading and resources at the end of this book. The problem, as I see it, is that this training is no longer *de rigueur*. Sloppiness and misinformation abounds. I believe there are many reasons for this, not the least of which is the fact that gifts aren't bestowed on an equal footing. Whether or not one is psychic, whether or not one has a specific talent depends far more on genetics and inheritance than personal worth. This truth is often viewed with distaste by modern folk who believe that any psychic experience should be open to anyone. I also think that we live in an age of instant gratification and actively training the gifts (or coaxing a latent gift to open) takes much more hard work and, Gods forbid, discipline than the average person is willing to expend. It's much more self-gratifying to indulge in feel-good metaphysics that have little to no effective application in the physical world at large, and to be honest, your average person can afford to do so. Those who actually have psi-talents cannot.

As a practicing magician, I've also chosen to include techniques that can help ward against magical attack. While not the primary focus of this book, the exercises provided are simple enough that even the most elementary practitioner can utilize them effectively. Since those with psi-talents are more likely than not to also have some sensitivity to magic and magical energies, it seems only sensible to touch on a few basic precautions that can aid in creating safety, both of oneself and one's home. There's no reason, by the way, why a person without psi-talent (and totally uninterested in developing it) couldn't find some benefit in the basic exercises given in this book. They're excellent meditational tools.

It is my hope in writing this book that I'll be providing my readers with the type of book that I desperately longed for as a teenager and young adult (and even now, when one of my students asks for good, basic reading material). In these pages, I share twenty years of personal experience both in training psi-talents, and in learning to control and master my own. The exercises given in this book are useful on many fronts, not just for the psychic. They are also indispensable for the occultist or practicing magician and for the Pagan or Heathen wishing to develop either ritual skills or a devotional practice (many of the basic exercises aid in stilling the mind and in learning to sense energy, including the energy of a Deity's presence). There is much crossover in applicability. If this book spares even one reader the pain and struggle that I myself went through, then I have done my job.

S. REICHER
MARCH 3, 2008
NEW YORK CITY

Part 1:

Basic Exercises

Back to Basics

We're going to begin with the most basic and utterly essential exercises for anyone interested in developing their gifts, engaging in devotional practice, learning to practice magic, or learning to work with energy. Regardless of whether or not you are a practicing magician, or even whether you are Pagan/Heathen, pretty much everyone can benefit from these exercises. If you interact with people in any way, shape or form during the day, you will at some point be influenced by their energy and emotional state. Now we can't generally *see* such energy (unless one has the gift of energy Sight), but we can't see germs either with the naked eye, and yet no one disputes their ability to affect us. Energy is everywhere in everything. Emotions, for example, are energy. How many times have you walked into a room in which two people have just had a terrible argument and felt the pall in the room? Perhaps it made you uncomfortable, or agitated. This is normal. Our bodies, whether we will it or no, respond to such unseen stimuli even if a person is otherwise generally psi-null. They can affect our mood and our stress levels, and even our overall health.

The exercises given in this chapter help mitigate the effects of such psychic "contamination". This is your first line of defense against imbalances in the etheric body and the first act of prevention necessary to maintaining a healthy psyche and body. Such imbalances can eventually affect one's physical and mental health. Many of these exercises are equally helpful in times of emotional upset and turmoil, and all of them are excellent stress reducers. For those who may be psychically talented, they are an absolute necessity.

In many respects, these basic exercises are like martial-arts training. When one practices in a martial arts class, the structured movements reinforce every technique that the student is learning in class. Many of the forms were passed down from generation to generation largely unchanged. They train both the mind and body, developing a kinetic memory and slowly strengthening the muscles and reflexes. These basic psychic exercises do exactly the same thing: they hone and strengthen mental and intuitive abilities. They put you in control of your gifts rather than the other way around. They also assist in effectively managing the potentially overwhelming stimuli that constantly bombards us from every quarter whether we are psychic or not. We are beings of energy: molecules in motion, and these techniques provide basic skills for keeping that energy in top form.

As with medicine, an ounce of prevention is worth a pound of cure, so before we delve into the realm of shielding and warding, attack and counter-attack, it's necessary to first master those exercises that will prevent 99% of most esoteric harm.

Centering

The first and most important exercise that one can do, be it to develop one's gifts or to begin one's spiritual journey, is centering— followed closely and equally by grounding. These two exercises go hand in hand and are the backbone of any spiritual and magical practice. They still the mind, make one aware of the flow of energy in one's body, give control over that energy and in the end bring an inner stillness that allows one to hear the voice of the Gods. They also lay the foundation for effective psychic and energy shields.

Centering and grounding are the most essential exercises you will ever learn. They should, ideally be done at least once a day and preferably twice. I generally recommend a minimum of fifteen minutes in the morning and again right before bed. Checking one's 'ground' throughout the day at regular intervals is not a bad idea either, especially as one is first learning the exercise. There are numerous ways to go about both centering and grounding. I tend to like to start people off with breathing exercises. The most common exercises given in most books tend to be visualizations, but not everyone (especially empaths) can visualize well. I prefer to start people with something a little more kinetic; I myself was a very kinetic learner who was constantly frustrated by the emphasis on visual techniques when I was first learning! There are many different ways to go about both exercises though. The important thing is to actually *do* them!

Centering should come before grounding, and basically means making sure that your physical, etheric/astral and auric bodies all occupy exactly the same space. This has to be done before the energy channels in the body can be properly aligned to best facilitate grounding. Centering is not difficult. The first exercise and the one that I consider the best is one that I originally learned in a martial arts class. It has many uses and best of all is very, very simple. All you do is focus on your breathing. Taking slow, even breaths, inhale four counts, hold four counts, exhale four counts, hold four counts. That's all. Do it over and over repeating the pattern without breaks. Try to time it to your heartbeat, but if that is too distracting, don't worry about it and just breathe. In time, you want to feel all the breath, all the excess, scattered, or jangled energy in your body gathering about three inches below your navel. This is your second chakra. A chakra is a nexus of energy in the body, and the word comes from the Sanskrit for 'wheel'. We can't see them (unless we have the gift of Sight) but they impact the energy of our body. There are seven major ones. While not everyone works with chakras, I'm partial to them, as the very first centering exercise I ever learned involved chakra work. Eventually, as you breathe, you want to feel and/or see the energy gathering in a glowing golden ball at this chakra. Basically, centering is "contemplating your navel"—mindfully, that is. Be sure to breathe through your diaphragm, taking deep even breaths.

Centering can be very calming when under stress. If you find yourself in an emotionally stressful situation, it may help to fall into this breathing pattern. There are, of course, many ways to center, but this tends to be the easiest and most adaptable. One's center is based on where one's center of gravity is. For most women, that is in the hips, the second chakra area. Some larger or large-busted women and most men center at the solar plexus (third chakra) or in some cases even higher. I don't recommend using any chakra but the second chakra or the solar plexus for this exercise though.

Grounding

Once the excess energy in your body has been collected, it has to go somewhere. Grounding adds stability by giving one a connection to the earth. Basically grounding is just sending all the excess energy that has been collected in the body down into the earth. Grounding provides both a stabilizing system of energetic 'roots' and a shunt for excess energies in the body. It also creates a tap-root, or line by which one can replenish one's energies when they run low. It is even more important, in my opinion, than centering. Grounding isn't hard either. It's occasionally boring, but not difficult.

The basic grounding exercise that's usually given is a good one. It entails feeling a cord of energy extending from your perineum (or root chakra) into the earth, reaching deeper and deeper and rooting you strongly. What most people won't tell you is that cord should be a double conduit: one half should allow you to send energy down, while the other allows you to draw energy up (or create two separate cords). There's a reason for this that comes into play if one is very magically active. If you get hit with an excessive amount of energy, you need to be able to dump it through that shunt very quickly or you'll get what's called a 'reaction' headache. You can't do that if you're using the same channel to draw energy up into you at the same time you wish to send something down.

The easiest exercise to begin with is also best when keyed to breath. Inhale and feel the energy gathered in your center. Now, as you exhale, feel that energy exiting the body through the perineum. On the second exhale, feel it entering the earth and branching out into a thick, sturdy network of roots. Continue this imagery for as long as you need to, with each ensuing exhalation taking you further and further into the earth until you feel fully grounded. While one can ground in multiple places (and this will be discussed a little later), the most important ground of all is the one here on Earth. Ground your awareness and energy cord right into the soil, into the land beneath where you're sitting, standing or walking. You have a right to this ground. You have a right to the connection to this soil. It is yours by right of birth. Knowing that, consciously and to the marrow of your bones, makes this process a thousand times easier. It is that awareness which must inform your grounding.

In many occult books, particularly ones that speak in depth about astral projection, one will often read about the silver cord that attaches the soul to the body and which can sometimes be seen when one astrally projects. This grounding cord that one creates through the exercise given above is just as vital. There is another occult maxim: As above, so below. It is the natural complement. In time you will want to learn different ways of grounding, and you will find that many of the exercises are primarily visualization exercises. Don't worry if you're not good at visualizing things...that too is a skill that comes in time. I struggled with it for many years. You may find that the image comes via feelings instead of sight, and that's fine. Don't worry if you can't see or feel anything....start with the mental focus and eventually your awareness of the internal flow of energy will increase. Energy follows awareness. Awareness follows imagination disciplined to will. Create the "groove" in your mind through daily, repetitive practice and eventually that groove will be created in fact, in one's energy, astral and etheric bodies.

My first teacher wasn't particularly visually oriented either, and taught me that the centering breathing pattern can also help with grounding. I've also often found it difficult to ground in airplanes and trains, so my colleagues and good friends in Clan Tashlin taught me a specific grounding to combat this that they refer to as the "Little Prince" exercise. Picture yourself standing upon the planet earth. See yourself as small, very small, the size of an ant surrounded and engulfed by the enormous, massive body of the earth itself. If you can put yourself in that experience viscerally, it will automatically ground a person effectively.

On an amusing but effective note, grounding can be likened to peeing out what bothers you. You gather all the upsetting, jagged, excessive energy in your body and send it out through the root. Gather all toxins that may have come from without, including negative emotions and energetically pee them out. That's grounding.

In addition to meditation and visualization techniques, it is also possible to use natural substances like stones and herbs to ground. This does not in any way take the place of regular grounding practice. It is a stop-gap technique to use in times of extreme need. One of the best grounding stones I know of is hematite. Tiger iron also works very, very well, but I tend to favor hematite as it is somewhat more readily available. It is absolutely one of the strongest grounding stones I have ever encountered. Energy-wise, it's very dense and heavy, which makes it the ideal tool for a student who is having problems grounding to focus on. (I have one student who cannot use this stone as it is so dense that she feels suffocated when linking into its energy.)

All living things have energy, and that energy resonates at different frequencies, depending on the stone, herb, etc. By aligning one's internal energies with that of a specific stone, one can bring about various desired changes – for instance, using hematite for grounding. A good meditation is to sit while holding a chosen stone in one's hand, focus one's breath into the stone, and slowly align one's internal energies to the same frequency of the stone. There are times that everyone has trouble grounding and centering, but this exercise can help alleviate some of the problems. Just sit and breathe, concentrating on how the stone feels and how it makes you feel when you hold it. Notice temperature, weight, emotions, images...anything that comes to mind.

Another use for hematite (or any chosen stone), one that is seldom mentioned in occult books anymore, is that of making elixirs and imbuing tea or water with the qualities of the stone. It's one way of internally cleansing what a bath or rubdown would take care of externally. It can be used, in conjunction with the techniques given above to aid in grounding or any other working. I would not use it by itself, and it does not substitute in any way for regular practice. Obviously some degree of knowledge about herbs is required for safety's sake. I would suggest, if not taking a class in medicinal herbology, possibly picking up either Maude Grieve's *A Modern Herbal* or the *Physician's Desk Reference for Herbal Medicine* as a reference. Below are two simple recipes for a grounding elixir. One part equals about one teaspoon.

Grounding Elixir #1

> 2 parts dandelion
> 1 part violet
> 1 part yarrow
> 1 part red clover

Make an infusion of this tea. This is done by pouring boiling water over the herbs and allowing it to sit for roughly 20 minutes. Then strain it into a bottle. (If you are planning on keeping this for a long time, make a tincture rather than an infusion. This is done by allowing the herbs to sit in a bottle of high proof vodka for a minimum of six weeks before straining. Tinctures need not be refrigerated and will keep for months. Usually when making tinctures, one part equals one ounce of the requisite herbs). Place a piece of hematite into the bottle and let sit for at least 24 hours (refrigerated).

A glass of this tea may be drunk whenever you practice your grounding. Herbal medicines can be prepared by tincture and/or infusion as well, but magical elixirs are not meant to be used for medicinal purposes.

Grounding Elixir #2

> 2 parts red clover
> 1 part ginseng
> 1 part betony
> 1 cross stone

Make a tea of the herbs via infusion. Strain and bottle. Add the stone refrigerate. Wait at least 24 hours before using. Again, none of these elixirs or stones substitute in *any way* for daily grounding and centering.

Reaction Headaches

One of the reasons that grounding and centering are so important to psychics and magicians is that they prevent and protect against something called a reaction headache. These are vicious and nasty things, caused by two things: either one has overworked oneself psychically/magically, or one has suddenly been bombarded with too much energy too quickly. Conversely, one can expend too much energy too quickly as well, which can cause the same unpleasant effect. Reaction headaches can be a sign that the body's energy channels have been completely overloaded. This can result in migraine, nausea, dizziness, sore muscles and, in extreme cases, shock. Having a good, solid ground is the best means of prevention. How will you know when you have a reaction headache? You'll know and it only takes one. Most students experience this at least once in their training. The milder forms can be a response to overworking the gifts. Energy overload, which can lead to reaction headaches, can also manifest as hyperactivity and giddiness rather than exhaustion and nausea. Be aware and on the lookout for either response.

Quick Fix Grounding Techniques

None of these "quick fix" techniques substitute for daily, disciplined practice. Repetition is the mother of learning, so I'll say it often: ground, ground, ground. I've yet to have a student who doesn't get bored with grounding far before it's truly mastered. However, there are times of emergency where one needs to ground very quickly, more quickly than one's skill will allow. Sometimes too, circumstances intervene to make regular grounding difficult. Here are a few things one can do until one has the opportunity and ability to effectively ground, which should be done as soon as possible.

1. Have a full meal, preferably with a good deal of protein. Food and the process of digesting are, in and of themselves, mildly grounding.
2. Unpleasant but very effective: Have someone pour a gallon of very cold water over your head. It snaps one's awareness back into the physical body like nothing else. It is particular good if one is having trouble coming out of any type of trance state. This is something to keep in mind for emergency situations.
3. Bathe or shower and change clothes. This has much the same effect as number 2, but in a far less jolting way.
4. Have a more experienced person ground you. Some energy workers and psychics have the ability to ground other people. It depends on their individual talents but any well-trained person should be able to do it.
5. Some people find sex very grounding; for others it has exactly the opposite effect. Use your best judgment here.

Cleansing Chakras

This is a more elaborate method of centering, and I believe it's generally good to do this at least once a week. This exercise entails cleansing each of the seven main chakras and then aligning them for a free flow of energy. The very first meditation exercise I ever learned (given below) dealt with the charkas, and I've found nothing better for regular energy maintenance. There are numerous other chakra points in the body other than these seven, but when dealing with occult matters, it's the primary seven that lie along the body's axis that we are mostly concerned with. I occasionally also perform this exercise incorporating two other chakras that lie above the crown, and two that lie below the root. Once you've grown comfortable with the exercise as given, feel free to do the same.

As I noted above, there are seven main chakras in the body and they can impact one's physical, emotional, and psychic health and/or create blockages that impact one's spiritual journey. Therefore, it is necessary to keep them clean and well balanced. Now a lot of what I'm telling you in this section may be a bit overwhelming, so in the beginning, just do your best with the exercises and eventually they will click into place.

Below is a chart giving correspondences for each of the chakras. This may help in your work with them. You don't have to memorize this; in time you'll discover your own correspondences. It's just helpful information to have. I have seen other, perhaps more traditional correspondences, particularly of color given to each of the chakras but this is the system that I learned twenty years ago and the one that I feel competent in teaching.

Chakra	Location	Color	It governs...	Element
Root	Perineum	Red	Survival, material support, health	Earth
Sex	3" below the navel	Orange	Desire, self image, self confidence	Water
Solar Plexus	Below the breastbone	Yellow	Self-mastery, will, motivation	Fire
Heart	Center of the chest	Green or pink	Emotions, love, loss, compassion	Air
Throat	Bottom of the Neck	Blue	Expression, communication	Sound
Third Eye	Between the brows	Indigo or white	Magic and psychic gifts	Ki (Chi)
Crown	Crown of the head	Purple	Wisdom, Divine connection	Divinity

The following exercise is a good way to not only clean one's chakras but to increase one's ability at visualization. When you do these exercises, be certain to inhale the energy in through the front of your body, the front of the chakra and exhale through the back! The chakras penetrate the entire body and have a front and back. If you like, you can expand upon this exercise by working up the front of the body and down the back. I have found that to be a particularly effective variation.

1. First, ground and center just like in the exercises given above. That's always the first thing you want to do.

2. Begin to focus on your root chakra. Inhale drawing energy/breath in through the root.

3. Exhale, sending that energy out. As you exhale feel all the blockages and dreck that might be clouding that chakra flow away with the breath. The chakras should, ideally, be about three inches in diameter.

4. Continue this for about a dozen exhalations, then begin to visualize a small seed of glowing red light pulsing in the center of the root chakra. With each inhalation, the red light grows brighter, and larger until finally it fills the entire chakra, pulsing and whirling and spinning.

5. When you feel that this chakra is opened and cleansed, turn your attention to the second chakra, the sex chakra.

6. Do exactly the same thing, but when you exhale, send the energy out through the back of the chakra and of course you will visualize a glowing orange light.

7. Continue this exercise up all the chakras until you reach the crown using the appropriate color for each chakra (i.e. solar plexus: yellow, heart: green, throat: blue, third eye: indigo, crown: royal purple).

8. Once you have reached the crown, return your attention to the root. Inhale, drawing energy up through the root. As you exhale, allow that energy to travel through the chakras, to burst from the crown and cascade around you like the branches of a weeping willow tree. This energy flows back into the earth.

9. Do this at least six to twelve times, then in reverse, pulling energy in through the crown and allowing it to travel down to the root and into the earth. Do this six to twelve times as well.

10. After this, ground as much as you feel you need to and have a little to eat.

Advanced Grounding Techniques

You've already learned a very basic grounding exercise, and now we're going to take that to the next level. There is much, much more to grounding than learning to "be a tree", though that particular visualization is still, I believe, the best place to start. That being said, such a simplistic exercise may be fine for a beginner but will not afford adequate protection from psychic or magical attack, nor will it serve one well in many modes of energy work. Once the basic exercise has been mastered, it's time to expand the premise into a ground suitable for magic, combat and extensive gift work.

When I was initially taught to ground, I was told that one's ground is a two way channel—a person can pull energy up just as easily as he or she can send energy down—and that this was a foundational practice in many forms of energy healing and energy work. Well, yes and no. Firstly, it is best to have a ground into which you can root energy and another established channel through which you can draw energy up. I also recommend establishing multiple shunts through which you can quickly disperse large amounts of incoming energy. You can quickly see why the idea of a root system of a tree is so effective! As noted before, the reason one should not use one's primary ground to also pull energy in is because if you suddenly need to dump energy and your ground is already occupied with drawing energy up, you're screwed. Energy backlash is a nasty thing. It can lead to nausea, shock, migraines, fainting and complete electrolyte disruption. Ideally, one's ground should be multifaceted, with at least one channel being utilized specifically to draw energy back into the body.

I'm a Norse practitioner, so I tend to default to Norse cosmology in my work. Feel free to adapt this exercise to your own cosmology. We're initially taught to ground in the earth of Midgard, which is the land we stand upon, and this is the most essential ground one can establish. It is very important for stability and safety that this be established first, before any other kind of ground; I would go so far as to say that one should work regularly (i.e. daily) for at least a year using only a Midgard ground. Once you have created a solid ground in the earth, begin working on grounding in two places at once. If you were a Norse practitioner, you might work towards grounding both in Midgard and in Yggdrasil, the World Tree.

Norse cosmology has nine worlds, and each world has different beings, elements and power associated with it. Yggdrasil is the world Tree that supports the entire structure. Three good and useful books on Norse cosmology are *Exploring the Northern Tradition* by Galina Krasskova, *Pathwalker's Guide to the Nine Worlds* by Raven Kaldera, and *Essential Asatru* by Diana Paxson. These will provide a more in-depth study of the cosmology, but one should feel free to adapt this exercise to one's own cosmology as needed. Please do not attempt to ground in any world where you have not traveled astrally, and where you do not have permission from the denizens there.

Once you have successfully managed to ground in Midgard and at a second world, try to ground in three—say, Midgard, the World Tree and the Land of the Dead, for example. Make sure each grounding channel is of equal strength and stability, and take some time to experience and note how that feels and how it's different from a single grounding thread. One can actually ground in any of the nine worlds, and a *very* advanced exercise (and it is likely you will need permission from within each world to do this) involves extending a two-way ground into the earth and then one to each of the nine worlds all at the same time.

It is also possible to ground in Ginungagap, the primal Void, though this is *extremely* dangerous and should only be attempted when one has mastered grounding in all nine worlds, if at all. I know experienced magicians who blanch at the thought. The Void can take from you far more than you can take from it, and far faster than you realize. To quote a friend of mine: "Midgard is where you live, the body you live in, the feelings you have, what you think and what you do, how you feel about yourself and your life. It is your subjective reality." Losing one's temporal ground, one's Midgard ground means that no other ground will be truly stable. Grounding in the void means grounding in a place so primal that one could easily be sucked in and destroyed unless one's Midgard ground is of equal strength, and this can be a surprisingly difficult thing when balanced against the void with its almost irresistible pull. There may be times when one may temporarily want to ground here, but one should only do so after extensive experience and only when absolutely necessary.

To recap the advanced exercise:

1. Establish a good Midgard ground in the earth itself. Be a tree.
2. Establish a second channel through which you can draw energy up. If you like, a useful exercise is cycling energy into and out of the body in a continual cycle through these two channels.
3. Check your Midgard ground.
4. If that ground is solid, extend another grounding chord into Yggdrasil.
5. Balance out the two grounds, making sure they're of equal strength. It's OK if Midgard is a little stronger.
6. Check both grounds.
7. Extend a third channel into one of the nine worlds.
8. Balance out all three grounds.
9. Create at least two smaller channels, shunts either into Midgard soil or into the Tree through which you can quickly send incoming energy if you need to.
10. Balance out all of the groundings by drawing energy up and sending it back down to make sure they are all stable and of reasonably equal strength.
11. Once this has been done, you can begin to layer on shields and wards, which are discussed in subsequent sections of this book.

It can be very interesting to ground in the ocean as well, or any other element (rooting yourself in a mountain can be a very intense grounding experience), but I've never found that to be quite as stable as grounding in the earth, save for extending one's earth ground so far down that it touches the earth's molten core. That can be extremely effective, particularly when you need to rid yourself of unpleasant energies. The fire can purify them.

Mindgift Training and Management

Though not related to the faith directly, this is a topic of intense interest for many Neo-Pagans. In fact, some people are first drawn to the various Pagan traditions with the erroneous idea that it is all about magic and virtuosity of the mind. It is true that the spiritual work that we do can often catalyst rapid growth of mind talents (which will be discussed below) and lead to a growing awareness of natural energies, but there is a huge difference between magic, psi-talents and faith.

Perhaps the most prevalent fallacy currently in vogue is the idea of magic as religion. It is not. Magic is the art of harnessing natural energies through the conduit of will, gift, and body to manifest one's will on the material plane. It is the raw manipulation of power. It is the magician and the magician alone who is responsible for the outcome, and that outcome is generally based on focus, will and skill. Religion, on the other hand, is worship of the Divine Forces: Goddesses and Gods. Prayer is not magic. That is not to say that the two cannot be combined; magic is a gift of the Gods and as such may certainly find its place in ritual (and I've often had various Gods decide to "lend a hand" to many of my runic divinations); however, it is not in itself faith. When one prays, one does not generally know the outcome—that is in the hands and wisdom of the Deity in question. However, when one casts magic, the outcome may confidently be predicted within a varied set of parameters dependent on the level and power of the caster. To worship is to seek communion with the Gods; to act as a magician is to seek to act as a god. One could say that magic and its related Art of alchemy are the links between science and religion. Psi-talents are another thing altogether. They are inborn gifts, channels in the matrix of the mind that grant specific perceptive abilities.

Which presents the next point: All magic is about power. That is perhaps the most difficult thing for the aspiring magician to admit: All magic users take up the study of the Art because they desire power, and to bring their world into compliance with their desires and wills. There is nothing wrong with this. The judicious practitioner is guided by the knowledge that the Universe must always remain in balance, otherwise it brings destruction to the magician. "Evil" magics warp the web of fate and existence, but power itself is not evil. It is a tool, neither good nor bad. The only evil may lie in the intent of the caster and that itself is not magic, but ethics. The wise magician aspires to the power of a god all the while knowing that he or she is not God.

Honore de Balzac wrote that *Power is not revealed by striking hard or striking often, but by striking true.* That more than anything else describes the path of the magic user. Psychic abilities like telepathy, empathy (the ability to sense other people's emotions intimately), foresight, energy-sight and the like are inherent gifts often passed from one generation to another. Magic is an act of will and the conscious manipulation of natural energies. Of course, it goes without saying that the psychic talents make it that much easier to sense and work these natural energies.

For now, let's focus on the mind gifts. I want to make it very clear that these are *not* in and of themselves magic. There are many variations on these gifts, and each person will experience them somewhat differently but for all that, the basic gift training remains the same. There are three important factors to remember:

1. These gifts are normal and natural.
2. They often run in families, passing through the bloodline from one child to another, though again, many variations often appear depending on what gifts run in each parent's line. They are a genetic inheritance.
3. Like a physical muscle, they can be developed.

An active gift is one that is currently manifesting. You can use it, and it works. A latent gift is one that is not active and probably won't be without a great deal of hard work. It will, however, be passed onto one's children. A dormant gift is one that could very easily be triggered into awakening, or one that will naturally awaken with time and growth.

Generally, people will have one strong gift and one or two lesser talents. They can often be used together quite nicely and in the course of one's training, other gifts can open and develop. A very strong gift will inevitably be passed to one's children to some degree. This is why the same gifts tend to crop up in bloodlines over and over again. Some gifts like telepathy and empathy can be receptive or projective (meaning you may be able to send thoughts or receive them, sometimes both). I like to break the various talents down into the following groupings, and this is how they will be listed in this chapter.

Communication
  Empathy
  Telepathy
  Animal Telepathy
  Psychometry

Healing
  Empathy
  Physical Healing
  Mind Healing
  Land Healing

Physical Manifestation
  Telekinesis
  Pyrokinesis

Sight
  Precognition
  Postcognition
  Energy Sight
  Far-Sight/Remote Viewing
  Gift Catalyst

Miscellaneous
  Mediumship
  Null
  Tapping
  Generators
  Psychic Vampires

Grouping the gifts in such neat categories is actually somewhat problematic. They can bleed into each other quite strongly—a healer may be using a great deal of energy sight, or an empath may receive visual images solely through the emotional resonance.

The gifts of communication and sight are the most prevalent, to a greater or lesser degree. Each gift has certain dangers that must be guarded against, simply because one can become severely overwhelmed by the constant stimuli. This will be discussed below in the section on empathy.

Telepathy

The gifts of communication primarily involve some degree of telepathy. This is generally described as the ability to hear other people's thoughts, especially the surface thoughts. This is most common between partners, close family members, or friends, and in its lightest form can manifest in such ways as answering a question before it's voiced, plucking answers to questions seemingly out of nowhere, or knowing when a family member is thinking about you and wishing you would call. That is its simplest manifestation. Those with stronger ability in this area can read the surface thoughts of strangers, and with practice can learn to probe quite deeply. Crowds may be uncomfortable due to the "white noise" or pressure on the brain caused by the press of many thoughts and psyches, even when the gift isn't developed enough to tease out specific, individual thoughts. There are several ways that this gift can manifest: the ability to read thoughts to whatever degree; the ability to send thoughts to varying degree which can also manifest as the ability to strongly influence another person mentally; or both. Animal telepathy is similar, except that the gift is attuned to the higher frequency of animals rather than people. Generally if a person has one, he or she can develop the other.

Much of what is written about empathy can also be said of telepathy, except that the stimulus is emotional rather than thought-borne. It is very difficult to lie mind-to-mind, and a gifted telepath will usually be quite aware of when a person's words do not match thought and motivation. Most telepaths find a comfortable balance between shielding and swimming in the tide of incoming thoughts. It quickly becomes too exhausting to constantly shield every stray thought of every single person all of the time, so telepaths learn how much they can tolerate.

Any conscious effort on the telepath's part to probe another psyche deeply affects the probed entity, and requires a very deft touch. All people, gifted or not, have defenses in their psyches. It is necessary for the telepath to be aware of "mind-traps" if one practices conscious probing. The more that one uses telepathy, the more one can visualize the psyche as a landscape which can then be traversed. So, according to how one envisions that landscape, mind-traps can be rooms that one walks into with doors slamming, or pools of quicksand in which you must struggle to escape, or even a physical blow to the mind. Sometimes one can go into a specific part of another's landscape that even the person who owns the psyche is unaware of; there is usually a great deal of pain or rage in those parts of the psyche and to enter them can create an onslaught of those emotions for the one doing the probing.

It is interesting that the gift crosses all nationalities and thoughts will translate automatically into the native language of the telepath. I have an acquaintance who is a fairly gifted telepath. He worked for many years in retail and would often interact with people who didn't speak English as part of his job. He had a gift for figuring out almost immediately what these non-English speakers wanted. His secret, of course, which I knew but his employer didn't, was that he was using telepathy.

Knowing empaths, it can be said that emotion tends to be truer than thoughts. To develop the gift of telepathy, one not only has to accurately read thoughts and the truth of those thoughts, but emotions as well. Telepaths read emotions in a far more detached manner than an empath would. Emotion can be observed rather than directly experienced, rather like reading a book. If thoughts are water, their importance to the psyche that is being read is felt from gentle waves to a tidal deluge. Emotions control the temperature of the water.

Shielding telepathy is, to my knowledge, best done by visualizing a wall within the mind that nothing can breach. The wall can be hard or flexible depending on the desires of the person building it, but it must be envisioned as completely protecting the mind and the channel for telepathy. I and many others doing this work envision the gift-channels as actual tubes within the matrix of the mind. (It's an effective visualization for shielding). All one has to do with empathy and telepathy is to shield the channel itself. Of course, this is easier said than done and this will be discussed in more depth in the sections on Shielding and Warding.

Empathy

Empathy is the ability to intimately experience, sense or read another's emotions. It is a strange gift, one that is often misunderstood, and this can be potentially devastating as it is the one psychic gift that links intimately into one's own emotional state. Where the gifts are concerned, empathy is defined as the ability to feel another person's emotions as though they are your own, to experience them directly and intimately. This is not to be confused with sympathy or the ability to relate strongly to someone's feelings. I have seen it theorized that empathy is a weak form of telepathy, but I have found them to be two totally different gifts with totally different resonances and, more importantly, two completely different channels within the matrix of the mind. To an empath, emotions are the primary sense, the fabric by which they experience the world at large and without proper training this can be somewhat traumatic. If thoughts are carried by strong emotion, the empath can indeed read them. However, far from being a form of telepathy, empathy generally twins with some degree of healing, though it is considered both a gift of healing and a gift of communication.

A friend of mine once gave me a tongue-in cheek definition of what it is like to be an empath: "You might be an empath if: you hate personal contact, have seriously contemplated becoming a hermit and living as far away from people as possible, have ever felt enraged, or like crying or laughing a split second after being totally calm and for no apparent reason (and this corresponds to someone new coming into your general vicinity), know upon first meeting a person whether they will be a friend, an acquaintance, or to stay the hell away 'cause they got weird vibes."

Now, humorous though this may be, that description is not far wrong.

Empathy can be a very lonely gift; for all that empaths experience a rich tapestry of emotions from others, that same gift can effectively cut them off from their own. Physical touch especially may become violating and painful: it is difficult to shield the gift during any physical contact no matter how inconsequential. The empath is exposed to the full spectrum of another's feelings, feelings often overlaid with thoughts or images. This brings up the most difficult problem regarding this gift: it is very easy for an empath, even one well trained, to become lost in the flood and turmoil of others' emotions. It is very easy to lose oneself. It goes without saying that this can lead to immense psychological disturbances, withdrawal from people, or even the development of what is called an "avoidant personality". One of the most devastating combinations of talents is empathy twinned with an extremely strong gift of mediumship; this stimuli can literally drive a person mad unless they have a very strong support group and are given proper training in grounding, centering and shielding very early on.

There are many different degrees of empathy, and once one starts working magically with any type of energy, that gift can radically strengthen. It is an incredible healing gift, usually (but not always) indicating either the gifts of physical healing or mind-healing. With physical healing, the empath is able to accurately sense energy blockages, tension and pain within the body; with mind-healing, he or she is able to sense/read/heal the very fabric of a traumatized or unbalanced mind, even to journey directly into a person's inner landscape to varying degrees depending on gift strength and skill. Most empaths, regardless of whether or not they also possess healing gifts, are able to soothe raw emotions and occasionally influence the emotional state of others. It is also an invaluable teaching tool and students should beware: It is difficult to lie convincingly to an empath; the nature of the gift is the ability to see beyond mere platitudes or masks.

The first indication that a person may be an empath is extreme sensitivity to or an unusual awareness of the emotions of others, without recourse to body language cues or verbal reference. Unfortunately, in magical practice, the emphasis is all too often on merely seeing energy rather than feeling it, when both are valid means of harnessing power. Indeed, at its stronger levels, empathy can grant its own type of sight. On the negative side, emotional overload can cause a plethora of symptoms up to and including physical shock. Emotions are held in the body, so on a lesser level ulcers, migraines and massive tension can result. Regardless of whether one is learning to use the gift for magic or healing, or simply training it as a means of survival, the means of mastering the gift are the same: grounding, centering and shielding. In fact, these three simple exercises are the foundations on which all magic or gift work is based, regardless of gift.

Psychometry

Psychometry is the ability to acquire information, read feelings and occasionally receive images related to places or things that one touches. It always involves a certain degree of empathy and usually (but not always) some degree of Sight as well.

Healing Gifts

Mind healing and physical healing are fairly self explanatory. The former is the ability to manipulate the threads of a person's psyche to bring about positive healing, and is almost always empathy-based. A gifted mind healer can actually "rewire" the patterns of a person's psyche.

A physical healer utilizes natural energy to heal the body. Some systems for energy healing, such as Reiki or Ch'i Gong, come with their own training and in some cases their own "implant", an astral modification that allows the use of that system, and is passed from a skilled practitioner to a beginner. However, the simplest and most basic form of energy healing is simply "laying on of hands". The would-be healer sits with a volunteer, lays their hands on an area that could use some work, and concentrates on sending specific energy. The drawbacks to this method are that you might "tint" the energy in the wrong way (for example, putting "warm" energy into an inflamed area that could use cooling), or that you might accidentally throw something out of balance. The healing "systems" avoid this issue, but not everyone is able to learn them (other gifts can interfere with using that flavor of energy) and not everyone is able to receive them well.

A gift-catalyst (and I would consider this a teaching as well as a healing gift) consciously or unconsciously uses either telepathy, empathy or mind healing to open and unlock a person's natural latent gifts. They tend to be very strong in either empathy, healing, or telepathy. They are also the best at identifying gifts, even latent ones, in others.

Telekinesis and Pyrokinesis

Gifts of physical manifestation are rare. This is compounded by the fact that when they do manifest, the negative reactions of those around them are traumatizing and make them consciously refuse to use it or develop it again. With gifts, it's often "use it or lose it", and that attitude will shut down the strongest of gifts in time. Some gifts include the ability to manifest one's energy very densely on the physical plane and thus impact it directly. There are two gifts that fall into this category: telekinesis and pyrokinesis.

Telekinesis is the ability to move objects with the mind. It often manifests first in adolescence, and is responsible for many reports of poltergeist activity. It will often manifest under times of emotional stress or upset. Those with this gift learn to consciously manipulate the electro-magnetic fields of things around them. The basic exercises that I was taught to begin training telekinesis are as follows:

1.   Take a set of dice. Focus on a specific number as you throw and, extending your will into and around the dice, attempt

to make them roll that number. Dice are easy even for the completely untrained person to manipulate this way.

2.   Secure a pinwheel so that it is standing vertically. Clear your mind and focus on the pinwheel and push with your mind so that it begins to spin. Try not to be attached to the outcome. Often persistent inability is just a matter of nervousness and "performance anxiety".

3.   Next take a small rubber ball. Set it on a flat surface and try to move it with your mind. After this, work up to larger objects.

Pyrokinesis is the ability to light and control fire and heat with the mind. Again, it is easiest to manifest at times of extreme emotion, and emotional balance is extremely important to one with this gift. A colleague of mine once told me that every single person he's known who could actively and consistently manifest this gift were in some way mentally unbalanced. I have not found this to be true, but it is worth considering. My colleague speculated that it had something to do with the fire energy coursing through the neuron-pathways of the brain. The one person I knew who could consistently do this was somewhat volatile emotionally, but otherwise perfectly sane and well-grounded. The gift would only manifest though at times of extreme anger, which is, in itself, an unbalanced state. Pyrokinesis can be dangerous to the bearer unless they learn early on to channel the excess energy into the earth (i.e. ground) and given how often this gift is tied to extreme emotions, learning emotional control is of utmost importance. There are a few exercises that I have learned over the years to help develop this gift:

1.   Light a candle. Clear your mind and focus on the candle flame. Try to actively affect it by moving it over to one side, then the other, making it higher, putting it out, all with your mind.

2.   Fill a clear bowl or glass with cold water. Focus on the glass. Focus on seeing the actual molecules that make up the water. When something gets hot, it's actually the result of molecules in motion. The molecular structure becomes agitated and heat is the result. So, focus on the water and heat it up, to boiling if you can.

3.   Focus on an unlit candle. Try to light it with your mind. Work up to larger fires. Always have a fire extinguisher near by.

Part of the effort with both of these gifts lies in finding the appropriate channel in your mind matrix and utilizing it properly. Things get much easier when you've achieved your goal once—then your unconscious mind realizes that it is, indeed possible and this removes a major psychic block.

There are no shielding techniques particularly useful against gifts of this family. If a telekinetic wants to move you, you will move. The only defense against these gifts is to attack them with a strong mind or empathic blast, thus destroying their center and keeping them off balance long enough to be taken out of commission. Both gifts tend to manifest primarily through line of sight although with practice this can change, especially if the gifted also has one of the gifts of sight.

Gifts of Sight

The gifts of sight fall into four categories: pre-cog, post-cog, far-sight and energy sight. Precognition (or pre-cog) and post-cog are essentially flip sides of each other.

Foresight, or precog, is the ability to read the future. It can manifest many different ways depending on the strength of the gift.. Diviners often develop a degree of this, in the ability to read the fluctuations of the cosmos. Essentially foresight has four primary manifestations:

1. Simple intuition: a feeling, a knowing that something will occur. This can strengthen through contact if one is empathic or as the time of the incident draws closer.
2. Ability to read the threads of *wyrd* (fate), seeing all the various possibilities at once consciously.
3. Strong visions of what is to come, usually of incidents surrounded by strong emotion.
4. Dreams of future occurrences.

This can be a very difficult gift to accept, and very disturbing, as the most common visions are usually negative (because there will be the strongest emotion surrounding them). This gift twins extremely well with empathy, as images are often carried by emotion and it is actions taken from emotional motivation that most often affect the *wyrd* web. The important thing to remember is that the future is not set; seeing something does not make it happen. A useful technique is to learn detachment from the images or visions, watching them flow past like images on a movie screen. With a very strong gift, however, these visions can be a total sensory experience in which this will not be possible. Lighter versions of this gift most often manifest in very subtle ways, like knowing exactly who is on the phone before you pick it up, without Caller ID. Reading Tarot will strengthen this gift, as will rune work. If the gift manifests in dreams, keeping a dream journal is often a useful practice.

There can be very little warning before this gift kicks in, and the dreams or visions will come with little preparation and this cannot be shielded against. As with all the gifts in this category, the acceptable level of their influence in the environment is often more difficult to ascertain, which will be frustrating for the person who has the gift. Each foreseer reaches a point of accepting other people's reactions to their gift, from total belief to complete denial. For people who are particularly gifted, the strength of the visions can be independent of any personal intimacy with the people involved in the seeing.

There are people in the world who are so naturally open to foresight that whoever has the gift in their presence just sees an unusual amount of future occurrences. These people are like transistors for the energy of the web. (If the gifted person has a very strong degree of projective empathy or telepathy, it may be possible to project images into the mind/consciousness of another. That would be very, very rare, but a useful defensive talent in a gift that is usually not defensive.) Especially in matters of death among loved ones, having a foreseeing could change the gifted person's reaction if the death actually occurs. They would go through the grieving process at the point of the seeing rather than the actual happening.

Post-cognition is foresight in reverse. One may get images of the past, especially from objects or certain places; this gift does often blend into psychometry. This can manifest in the exact same way as foresight and one can also read past deeds of people. Again, the consciousness will be drawn to incidents surrounded by extreme emotion, which leaves a psychic imprint. Farsight, or remote viewing, is the ability to see happenings in a location in real-time, far from one's actual physical location. Again, the sight may be drawn to emotions but this is not always so. Astral projection is very easy for those with even a hint of this gift, as is lucid dreaming. I'm in no way a seer, but I have picked up a few exercises over the years that may prove useful to those of you who are:

1. Take a deck of playing cards. Take each card face down and run your hands over it. Go through the deck trying to determine color. When you reach 100% accuracy, do it again for suit. When you're accurate at that, try to guess what each card is: suit, number, court, etc. This can be done with Tarot cards too with equal efficacy. If you have a partner to practice with, you can have your partner look at the card and then you write down what it is without your partner telling you. It should be noted that neither of these exercises is pure sight. The first incorporates a touch of psychometry and the latter, a touch of telepathy.

2. Learn to read Tarot. This is an excellent way to train and develop precognition. The cards are merely visual devices that allow the reader to key his or her conscious mind into their foresight. It's a way of surmounting our internal censors.
3. Keep a dream journal. This tends to be useful for seers of all types, who tend toward a facility for dreaming.

There are many books out there on how to achieve astral projection. While I have done this a number of times, I find it unpleasant; however, I was taught an exercise by which to develop this facility, so I pass it on here.

Fasting can be useful for this goal. It sounds odd, but the idea is to weaken the astral body's hold on the physical, so go on a liquid fast for a week. There is a skill to fasting. One should not simply begin a fast or break a fast. One should take as many days to go into a fast as one will actually be fasting. The same goes for breaking a fast. If you plan to fast for five days, then take five days to ease into it, decreasing your food intake little by little and take five days to bring yourself back up to solid food. (For the love of the Gods, do not break a fast by having a full meal! You'll seriously regret it). Not everyone can do a full fast and that's OK. If you have health issues, are on medication, or have any blood sugar issues, you should consult your physician before beginning a fast. If you cannot fully fast, that's okay. One can do a modified fast with less discomfort and achieve almost the same results. Cut all meat and animal protein, all sugar and all processed food out of your diet for a specified amount of time. Do the centering breathing exercise frequently during your fasting period.

There are other methods to aid in loosening the link between the astral and physical bodies, including sensory deprivation, long-term meditation, and even methodical pain. A full treatise on astral projection is, however, beyond the scope of this book. Check the resources at the end of the book for more information.

Energy sight is perhaps one of the most common forms of sight. It is the ability to see the flows of energy, magical energy, auras, elementals, noncorporeal beings, *vaettir* (spirits) or manifestations of Deity. It's an excellent gift for a magician to have. It's also very useful for healers, and most healers develop some degree of this gift in order to see the energy blockages of their patients. This gift often twins with mediumship. If the person has another gift, their sight will influence their perceptions of the energy resonances of that gift: if they are empaths, they won't only feel emotions but will see the emotional energy in some form, and the same with telepaths. Most people have a touch of this gift, but a strong gift in another field may overpower it to the degree that it becomes very difficult to recognize.

For those who want to sharpen their dream abilities, working with a dream pillow can be somewhat helpful. I recommend the following recipe: Take two squares of dark cloth roughly six inches by six inches. Sew around three sides and affix a zipper to the fourth. Fill this pillow with the following herbs:

> 3 parts mugwort (this herb tends to bring clear, sharply lucid dreams all on its own)
> 1 part chamomile
> 1 part hops
> 1 part chapel flowers doused with jasmine oil (allow to dry thoroughly before adding)
> 1 part rose petals doused with rose oil (allow to dry thoroughly before adding)
> 1 part vervain
> A small amethyst

Sleep with this pillow near your face. Alternatively, you can use a pouch instead of a pillow and sleep with it near your head.

Mediumship

Mediumship most often twins with energy sight, and is the ability to hear, see and interact with noncorporeal beings. Not all mediums may be able to see spirits; some will hear them instead, using clairaudience instead of clairvoyance. Mediums are often so loosely anchored in their physical bodies that it is very easy for non-corporeal entities to come in and take over. It is the most seductively dangerous of the gifts, as mediums naturally lack a strong hold to the physical world. This is not a matter of will; rather, their astral bodies simply aren't particularly well grounded, and extra attention must be paid to the basic exercises. (I do not consider the ability to become possessed by the Gods or spirits necessarily mediumship. It is a unique gift or type of mental/neurological wiring in and of itself.)

It is important for active mediums to realize that spirits and other entities of the noncorporeal nature can be as annoyingly ignorant as humans. Death does not confer great wisdom. Don't always take what a spirit says as truth; they can be deceitful, so be careful. Most mediums, if they're lucky, develop a very strong relationship with at least one or two positive spirits. They talk to them often and trust has been established on both sides. They usually practice the development of their gift with those particular spirits. I generally suggest working with one's ancestors to develop this gift. Opening oneself up to any spirit is always a risky venture, and the budding medium should try to have others present, especially those experienced and with sight, when developing this gift. A good rule of thumb is: don't call anything you can't banish. If it has glowing red eyes, it's bad. If there is a stench, it's bad. If what it's telling you seems too good to be true, or just what you want to hear, it's bad. If it seems all-knowing, be skeptical. Spirits will often be attracted to mediums because they need and want to communicate; this is especially true of ghosts. This isn't bad, but it can be draining, and it's perfectly okay to tell the spirits to come back later. As I once told a distraught medium, "Just because they're dead doesn't mean you have to talk to them."

One of the most profound experiences and duties of a medium is to aid the soul in its passage to the other side. Often mediums will find themselves strongly called by Deities of the underworld for just this reason. It is important for those without the gift not to put undue pressure on mediums to explain away all the mysteries of death just because they can see spirits, and it is important for mediums to resolve their own issues with death. Large natural or unnatural disasters can strongly affect mediums, as can locations where great disasters or tragedies have occurred.

In some religious practices, believers are trained to work within a specific system of experiencing these non-corporeal beings. Mediums should learn to recognize these systems and regard them as sacred. (One example would be Santeria. I would, for instance, suggest asking permission before chatting with their spirits.)

Mediumship can prepare one for divine possession, but it is generally *not* a good idea to invite anything other than Deity (or a spirit that is well-known to a religious system that you work with) to come in and take up residence. Sometimes when a Deity feels it is necessary, They will temporarily give one the ability to experience a gift that person doesn't necessarily possess. For example, if one must help a spirit and doesn't possess the gift of mediumship, but are the only possible source of aid in the area, asking a Deity for instructions can help. This can occasionally leave one with a newly opened gift-channel. The best way to learn to cope with this particular gift is to ground and center *ad nauseam et ad infinitum*. If the spirits that are communicating with you are deceased humans, and your own ancestors are willing to develop a relationship with you, they can be a source of aid. Talk to them, set up an ancestral altar with images, food offerings, candles, incense, glasses of fresh water, anything that piques your interest and intuition. If it is possible, make your own ancestors a part of your life. They can provide help and, more importantly protection. (Some people may be rejected by their ancestors for a variety of reasons.)

Nulls

Anybody with a gift may occasionally run into "nulls". Nulls are people who may or may not have a gift, but who are naturally resistant to the influence of a particular gift. Psychic gifts will not work in the presence of these people. It's the damnedest thing. They are extremely rare. They are very difficult for gifted people to be around, as they are not consciously shielding, but are almost totally unreadable. Often they are extremely gifted people who have developed naturally ironclad shields as a survival mechanism.

Tapping

Tapping is an extraordinarily rare gift; in all my years of teaching, I've only run into it twice. It's the ability to tap into someone else's mind-gifts, using them to either augment one's own gifts or to use as if one had that gift. Personally, I believe it is tied to being a gift catalyst, though it may be pure coincidence that the two people I knew who possessed tapping were also gift catalysts.

Generators

This is another rare gift. Some people are born with the ability to amp up other gifts, or to channel a great deal of energy into any working. It's as if they're psychic and energetic generators. They are often lacking in any other psi-talent (save for Sight; for some reason, generators tend to be Sighted) and often have a great deal of difficulty grounding, centering and really staying focused in the mundane world. Occasionally they can have a gift of mediumship. The problem with generators is that, like mediums, they're not really all that well connected to their physical bodies, and/or to the physical world. They tend to be rather flighty. They also tend to attract a great deal of unwelcome and occasionally dangerous attention specifically because the gift is so rare and its bearers often so pliable.

If you happen to be a generator, ground as though your life depended on it. Work hard to develop regular habits of centering, grounding and shielding and if you can afford it, study a martial art. The latter helps develop exquisite body awareness, is very grounding, and can provide a necessary and often otherwise lacking discipline.

Psychic Vampires

A psychic vampire is a person genetically wired to require *prana*, or life energy the way that non-psi-vampires require food. There is evidence in occult circles that this talent is genetic and tends to run in families much like the other psychic gifts. In brief, there are two types of psychic vampires, primary vampires who are born that way, and secondary vampires who either learn the skill as a survival mechanism somewhere along the way, or who are consciously modified via energy work. The best book out there on this particular talent, which is somewhat beyond the scope of this volume, is *The Ethical Psychic Vampire* by Raven Kaldera.

Primary psychic vampirism can be an extremely useful gift. Many can train up their abilities so that they can suck pain, depression, anger, sorrow out of people, gaining sustenance from the negative emotions while at the same time helping the person upon which they feed. They can often digest very negative, tainted, or unpleasant energies in a place or in things and can thus cleanse people, places, and things very effectively. There are drawbacks to having this particular talent, though, and certain caveats; for any readers who suspect that they might be or know a psi-vamp, I highly recommend Kaldera's book.

For each gift, there is a unique relationship with others who have the same gift. For some it's very comforting (I have found it to be so with empaths—it adds a whole new dimension by which one can communicate); for others it may be very jarring when together.

Across the board, I've also found that being around other psi-talented people, particularly those that share your own talent, can be very helpful in learning to develop it. Sometimes it's just a matter of being in an environment where you are seeing clearly that these things are A) accepted and B) possible that provides the inner confidence to actively manifest your gifts.

ling

After centering and grounding, the next important exercise that must be learned is that of shielding. Many people tend to use the terms "shielding" and "warding" interchangeably and indeed, I myself have been guilty of this on occasion as well. However, a ward is a protection placed on a place or thing, and a shield is a protection placed on a person; at least that is how I was taught to conceive of the difference.

Shields are necessary. We lock our doors when we go outside. We wear warm clothing in winter. We put on sunscreen when going to the beach. Shielding one's aura is exactly the same thing: good psychic common sense. It prevents a plethora of problems.

Again, everyone can learn these exercises. You don't have to be especially psychic to do them; they are for everyone and, in fact, most psychics I know would be painfully glad if everyone *did* learn these exercises! Walking around unshielded is like walking into a room full of thieves naked with your wallet and valuables in hand. To someone who is psi-talented, it's the equivalent of walking into a room screaming at full blast while wielding a sledgehammer. Learning to shield oneself is a matter not only of common sense but of simple psychic courtesy.

We're going to begin by discussing personal shields. These are shields, either mental or magical, that one raises to protect against outside influence or attack. Such shields are not just to protect against some magical attack that, for most people, won't ever come, but are essential for those with certain talents especially empathy and telepathy. They make the world bearable and prevent overstimulation of the senses, with the sickness that it can bring. They're also useful for people with minimal gifts as well. They will keep your emotions and thoughts from leaking, which in turn will help you better maintain your own emotional equilibrium. Not to mention that having mental shields will make you far more comfortable to be around for anyone who is empathic or telepathic. Energy shields, on the other hand, protect on a magical level what mental shields protect on a psychic level: they prevent unwanted energy from attaching to the aura or entering the sphere of one's physical/astral/etheric bodies and doing harm.

As you can see from this brief description, there are two necessary types of shields—mental gift shields and magical shields. One is constructed within the mind to shield specific gifts, and the other is constructed externally to shield from external energies and, if necessary, magical attack. Ideally, one should develop both independently from each other. A mental shield is not enough to protect against magical attack, nor is a magical shield enough to prevent against psi attack in many cases. With a little practice and concentration, even someone with a very low level of magical ability or gift can learn to maintain both types of working shields.

Shielding can be very complex. At advanced levels, a person will have various layers of shields which interlock, supporting and complementing each other. The idea, particularly with magical shields, is to construct a layered matrix that can withstand repeated battering without ever collapsing, one that cannot be easily breached. There is a caveat to all this shielding: the more complex the shield matrix, the easier it is for someone with strong psi or strong magic to tell that you know what you're doing. It advertises, in many cases, not only that you're someone with a strong gift, but that you know how to use it. This isn't always desirable. Therefore, it's useful to learn to camouflage one's shields. This is something that we'll be discussing in more detail below.

There are dozens of different types of shields and each one has its benefits and drawbacks. I'm going to talk about a few different types here, but do not feel that you must limit yourself to what I'm describing. Let's talk about psi-shields first.

First, it's important to point out that many of the gifts cannot be effectively warded, either by one who has them or against them by one who doesn't. Sight falls into the first category and telekinesis into the latter. Mental or psi shields are most important for empaths and telepaths for whom it can be very difficult to adequately function amongst people without them. Mediums require a combination of heavily grounded shielding that is both mental and magical, preferably tied together. Because emotions are energy, empaths ideally require both mental and energy shields.

There are two ways that I have learned to shield empathy or telepathy mentally. The most common type of mental shield given is this: in your mind, feel/see a wall (it can be as flexible or hard as you like) inside your head. This wall blocks or filters any incoming thoughts or emotions. It must be constructed through concentration of the mind and while it can take constant attention at first, in time, it will become secondary. A skilled telepath or empath can actually create complex and layered mental shields that filter, ward, and misdirect. I once encountered a skilled empath who had the equivalent of a labyrinth protecting that particular gift-channel. While he was still able to read with exceptional accuracy, this labyrinth of mental shields, almost an inner landscape if you will, provided him the necessary detachment to avoid feeling overwhelmed by his substantial gift.

The caveat with this type of shielding for empaths is that no matter how great the shielding, it is nearly impossible to shield against physical touch. In fact, I have seen empaths touch a person lightly to verify the honesty or accuracy of a statement. Most people may hardly be aware or able to admit what they're feeling at any given time, but the average empath is always exquisitely aware of his or her emotional state—and usually everyone else's in their general vicinity as well—and can tease out individual threads and shades of meaning from what the non-empath would characterize as one, blunt emotion. With another empath, simple touch can provide a means to project images or feelings, adding another powerful layer to the means by which they can communicate. Another caveat with shielding is that empaths may misread a shield as irritation or annoyance or even dislike. I know that I myself sometimes read exhaustion or illness as active irritation. This is why clear communication is essential.

A simpler method of shielding, but one that may feel very disconcerting, is to actually consciously plug the gift-channel. I have found it very helpful to conceive of the gift-channels as tubes or pipelines running through the matrix of the mind. One effectively puts a mental cover on the "pipe" that corresponds to empathy or telepathy respectively. This takes almost no energy, but will effectively block the gift almost completely, if it's done properly. I do not recommend keeping this type of shield up for more than a few hours or a day at most, as it is an energy drain. It is, however, very effective.

It's important to raise and maintain shields before you ever leave your house. If you are an unshielded empath or are keeping only weak shields up (and it may be necessary to check your shields several times a day for a long time to ensure that they are solid and strong) and then enter an emotionally heated situation or a large group of people, the sudden swelling press of emotion can be overwhelming and painful. Once external stimuli gets through one's shields, it is almost impossible to shield it out again without completely removing yourself from the situation that caused the breach. It is possible, in such a situation, for a more experienced magician or empath to extend shields over someone who's having shielding trouble but this is to be avoided if at all possible (and while magical shields don't substitute for good mental shields, in such a circumstance, they're better than nothing because they will disrupt incoming energies to some degree. Emotion is, to this way of thinking, energy).

Energy shielding is a bit more complex. Mental shields will *only* protect against thought and emotions, or empathic or telepathic probes or attacks. They will not in any way protect against magical attack. Conversely, magical shields will offer limited mental protection mentally while at the same time protecting against magical attack.

In order to shield, it is absolutely necessary to be strongly and deeply centered and grounded first. Without a solid center and ground, it is impossible to maintain a strong and stable shield matrix. Ideally, one should get to the point that maintaining that effective shield matrix is second nature. It's possible to set shields so that they are self feeding and more or less self maintaining, save for cleaning and repairs that will inevitably be necessary should they ever come under attack. The more energy sensitive one is, the easier it is to tailor shields to one's personal specification as opposed to simply having a bubble-like force-field, which is what people usually envision at first.

So what happens after you've correctly grounded and centered? Once you've established as strong a ground as possible, choose a power source. What this is depends on the type of shield you want to construct. Most people are taught to first draw energy from the earth, from one of the many lines of power that criss-cross beneath the surface. These are called ley lines, and the place where multiple lines meet is called a node. There are levels of these meridians throughout the land and when they are absent, it is usually a sign that the land is not healthy.

Ley lines are sensed through the art of dowsing, with rods or a pendulum (or for the very gifted, their own bodies). If you're interested in dowsing, it's best to find someone with this gift to assess and train you. (One source of information is the American Society of Dowsers, PO Box 24, Danville, VT 05828 USA.) To try sensing ley lines by yourself, walk across a large open natural space – preferably flat like a field, as it's easier for beginners – and try to extend your consciousness down into the earth. Feel for lines of energy, some wide as a bed, some narrow. Some have energy that flows up; others have energy that pulls down. We'll come back to ley lines in a moment; first, shield.

How to Shield:

1. Center and ground.
2. Find a power source.
3. Draw energy up around you.
4. Shape it to your will and need.
5. Make sure it has a power source upon which to feed.
6. Set it to the desired degree of porousness or hardness (envision or feel it to be so).
7. Make sure that it doesn't conflict with any other shields you may have. You want each layer of your shield matrix to integrate cleanly. In other words, they need to get along.

8. Project onto it a sample of what it's feeding on or repelling. Think of this as the equivalent of giving a blood hound the scent of its prey. Tell it strongly that *this* is what it is to watch for, or devour, or deflect, depending on how it's cast.

9. Check it occasionally to make sure it is strong, stable and hasn't accrued any tears or damage.

Or, simplified:

1. Build it.
2. Feed it.
3. Tell it what it's bouncing away.
4. Perform necessary maintenance.

Let's use ley lines as an example. Once you are properly centered and grounded, you want to extend your senses into the earth, reaching down with a tendril of consciousness—something like an invisible hand—until you touch a ley line. Draw energy up carefully, allowing it to flow around you shaping itself to your aura. Make sure that it forms a complete sphere: top and bottom both need to be shielded too. In fact, I also like to allow a shield to mold itself to my grounding channel. A skilled magician can strike at a person's ground, overloading it, if the ground is not also shielded. This is unpleasant.

If you can't sense it, "fake it 'til you make it" is the rule of the day. Remember, energy follows thought and thought follows imagination and all of this needs to be disciplined to one's will. The first shields that are usually taught to people are either bubble shields or mirror shields. They are both effective but also have their drawbacks.

Bubble Shields

This is a very easy, very basic shield to make and maintain. It can be set to be fairly viscous, or to filter as though a delicate net. It is, unlike many other shield types, fairly comfortable for non-psi people to be around, even when it is not camouflaged. (Sometimes people, even if they have next to no gift, will sense a shield and respond negatively to it. We'll be discussing this more fully in the section on camouflaging shields.) This is a nice shield for a beginner to maintain on a regular basis in addition to mental shields—they won't do anything to block telepathy, though.

To construct one, use the part of your grounding channel that allows you to draw energy up into you and draw up the necessary energy. Either bring the energy up around you in a bubble form (think of an egg) or bring the energy into your body and feel it expanding outward from your solar plexus until it completely encompasses you. Ideally, you want the shield to feel bouncy, as though anything thrown at it would bounce off. If you want to get particularly creative, visualize the energy to be a soothing color. I usually don't bother with this but it can affect the way people respond unconsciously to your shield. Usually I experience the energy as gold, particularly if it's drawn from earth.

Caveats: While this is a nice, comfortable and easy shield to make and maintain, it has absolutely no defensive applications whatsoever. It will not hold up to any type of serious attack.

Mirror Shields

As their name indicates, mirror shields are hard shields created to reflect any incoming attack. The external surface of the shield is usually envisioned as diamond-hard and mirrorlike.

This shield is constructed pretty much the same way a bubble shield is. You draw energy up around you (and I would suggest bringing the energy up around you rather than bringing it into you and projecting it out through the solar plexus for this particular shield, as this is a harder, sharper shield to manipulate) and shape it into a sphere. Make sure that it sits close to the aura; you don't need to have a huge, bold shield. Once you have your sphere created, focus on the external side. See/feel that side becoming diamond hard and reflective. I usually envision this shield as either hard silver, or diamond-like and clear.

I've occasionally slapped a mirror shield on students who couldn't control their gifts, except that I created the shield with the mirror on the inside so that everything they inadvertently projected was reflected immediately right back in their faces. This is not a nice thing to do, and only the contract that we'd entered into as teacher and student gave me the lawful right to do so.

Caveats: This shield is reflective. Incoming attacks will bounce off, if it's constructed properly. This means, just like a bullet ricocheting in a closed space, what bounces off can strike someone innocent. If this happens, you're responsible karmically for that harm. Also, this shield's surface is diamond-hard, but diamonds can be shattered if they're struck at the right point.

Elemental Shields

These are particularly powerful and good for layering. Elemental shields are rarely static like a mirror shield and this makes them incredibly flexible and strong; not to mention if cast correctly, they partake of the essence and power of the element they're drawn from. In magic, the four classical elements are wind, fire, water (or ice) and earth. The nature of a shield cast from an element will reflect the nature of the element itself. This is important to remember: in constructing the shields you must work within the boundaries of the element's nature itself. It helps if, as a magician, you have some hands on training with the four elements. Some direct understanding of their very physical power will help you connect more strongly to their magical essence.

Wind Shields

Imagine a tornado or raging hurricane winds. This is the power you want to infuse your shield with. When you call the energy up around you, you want to consciously imbue it with the nature of wind. Wind has its ley lines and currents, even nodes, just like the land does ("as above, so below", after all). If necessary, you can tap into this to achieve the desired pattern. It's not good to tie a shield to these nodes though. The energies of wind, water, and fire are very, very different from the energies of earth, and wind, at least, will not tolerate such a binding. If it sounds as though I am intimating that the elements are alive, that is precisely what I'm doing. The elements have consciousness, sentience if you will, though it's in no way like human sentience. This must be respected when drawing on their energies and natures.

So, draw the energy up around you and pattern it to wind energy. This can be done by making it feel to your senses the way wind feels, by achieving the same "frequency" of energy. If you have permission from the winds to snatch a wisp of true wind to add and power the shield, then all the better. See and feel it whirling around you. I suggest having at least two layers to any good wind shield: layers whose projective force goes in differing directions. Wind is incredibly powerful. It can destroy cities (tornados, hurricanes), it can wear away stone. In the same way, a well-constructed and maintained wind-shield can disperse or wear away incoming, hostile energies.

You will note that I continually emphasize "maintenance" when speaking of shields. There is a reason for this. Shields, even the best of them, must be subject to regular maintenance to stay clean and strong and solid. For beginners, this may mean checking them every hour, or even twice an hour. For more experienced practitioners, it may mean checking them once a month. However you choose to do it, don't just set a shield and forget about it forever. Look in on it, check it for energy leaks or holes. Do what you need to in order to keep it in good working order. This is your external security system, after all.

Fire Shields

Fire shields are cast in much the same way as wind, save that you are drawing on the essence of fire. Feel/see the flame enveloping you. You (or rather your aura) are the wick in the midst of the candle flame. The fire is the shield around your aura. The incoming emotions of others, and any hostile energies form the "oxygen" on which the fire feeds.

This is both an easy shield to maintain and an easy shield to build combat shields around. Fire is particularly useful in combat: it will just eat up whatever is thrown at it. (If too much is thrown, it can overload before devouring what is coming in, which is, as with any shield, a drawback.) This is also a fairly comfortable shield for others to be around. It is, predictably, warm. It can also look like part of one's aura, which makes it relatively easy to camouflage.

Of course, you can cloak yourself in a fire storm if you want, particularly if engaged in active combat. This is not something I'd suggest doing for every day though. When you need to strengthen the fire shield, do so by making the flames hotter and higher.

If you have a good working relationship with fire, you may be able to tie this shield into a cosmological fire world. Do not, however, try this technique without the proper permissions.

Water Shields

Drawing on the power of the ocean, the tidal wave, the flood, water makes an impressive and exceptionally powerful shield. There is no place water cannot go, which makes it an incredibly difficult shield to breach. Like wind and fire, this is not a static, solid shield. These elements are molecules moving in fluid states. There is nothing "still" about them.

Draw the water energy up with the roaring force of an ocean wave. Layer this shield. Let one layer wash over you, moving in a circular motion around your auric body from one direction, then raise a second shield to do the same from another direction. If you have a good working relationship with water, you may be able to tie this into a body of water itself, but that is a very individual thing. That perpetual motion is the shield itself. This shield usually feels cool and cleansing to the person casting it.

Ice Shields

Not everyone can work with ice. I happen to like the feel of this shield, but it can feel cold and remote to those outside its protection. You can set an ice shield by drawing on the nature of ice, by setting the shield frequency to "feel" like and "be" ice.

To make an ice shield, I draw upon the energies of the Norse world of ice, Niflheim. (Again, get permission from the denizens before tapping into another world.) From there I draw a shield of energy around myself. This is very like a bubble shield save that it is drawn of ice energy. I inform the shield that incoming energy is "heat". Ice will suck the warmth from that which is hot. Ice that is cold enough to sustain itself will freeze anything else. In this way, it devours incoming energy.

Earth Shield #1: The Sandstorm

Just as with the wind and water shields, this shield raises a swirling cone of energy around the auric body. In this case, that energy is constructed of earth energy, specifically that of a sandstorm. This is a very corrosive shield and will corrode and disperse incoming energy. I do not suggest having this shield next to your skin; it can feel rather abrasive.

Earth Shield #2: The Mountain Wall

For those who prefer shields that don't move, or for beginners for whom moving shields may be somewhat difficult, it is possible to draw upon the energies of earth to create a shield wall. This is a wall, thick and solid in feel as a mountain all around you. Anything that strikes it, will ideally, be stopped by the dense body of earth. You can, after all, fire a gun into a mountain without harming or in any way impacting the mountain itself. That is the idea here. Some people visualize this being build brick by brick like a wall, others feel the mountain rising around them. The drawback is that this is a heavy shield to maintain.

Spinning Vortex Shield

This shield is excellent in combat, but because of this, it's definitely a higher profile shield. Like the Wind Shield above, it's constantly in movement, spinning like a tornado around you. It functions by dispersing energy or deflecting it forcefully. It is cast by drawing up energy from one's ground. If you have a strong air affinity, you can pull energy right out of the air for this. That energy becomes a spinning vortex of raw force around your aura.

The benefit of this shield is that it doesn't require any elemental affinity. Its power comes from the utilization of pure force. It's very flexible and can be very easily combined with the firestorm, tornado, sandstorm or waterspout. The drawback is that it takes concentration and a great deal of energy to maintain. This is not an everyday shield.

Under-The-Skin Shields

In addition to external shields, there are ways of creating protections on and beneath the skin itself. I would not rely only on this type of protection, rather I would include it as part of a layered matrix if I chose to utilize these at all. I look at this type of shield as a last line of defense. It's backup protection to a well-constructed matrix of combat shields. It can be the last line of defense against magical attacks that include leech blades or darts (magic projectiles designed to suck one's life energy) and elfshot, a magically constructed weapon that will poison the blood and corrode the joints.

Draw energy up from the source of your choice. The grounding channel is good for this. Feel it filling your body, running like liquid just under the skin. Charge this energy, in whatever way is most comfortable for you: either as thin, flexible Kevlar, or a simple thin bubble...whatever you feel you can live with. I'd keep this simple.

You can do the same type of shield by drawing energy up through your ground, bringing it up through your center through each chakra until it reaches the crown. Exhale and send the energy out through the crown so that it rains down over your skin. Concentrate on getting a solid, even flow, allowing the energy to run over your skin, as close to the skin as possible. Then charge this on-the-skin armor: set it to be a densely packed, crackling energy field that will neutralize incoming energy. I recommend setting this particularly shield to remain latent until something hits your outer shield, at which point it can become active and "awake". This is done by mentally investing the energy with this knowledge and command as it is being cast.

It is also possible to create an emergency shield by changing the nature of your aura. I don't recommend this for daily use because it requires a tremendous amount of energy, but if you come under attack, you can actually harden your aura so that it repels incoming energy. This won't hold but thirty seconds or so; still, it's a useful emergency skill to have. Another useful trick is to make the aura viscous so that it traps incoming energy, then shed the aura like a snake sheds a skin. This can be uncomfortable but the aura will replenish itself.

Force Field/Disrupting Shields

This is a very useful shield to add to a layered matrix. It is not strong enough in and of itself to stand as a single shield, but added to a series of layers, it is very, very effective. The type of energy that works well for this is that of electricity, lightening, even energy from the Void (use this last ONLY if you are an experienced magician, as it can kill you otherwise) or anything that has an electrical charge to it. This is a very thin, very light shield; it can even be cast as a thin net that will disrupt the frequency of any incoming energy, thus dispersing its power. I personally like to use this as my second layer of shields, right beneath my concealment shield, which is the most external layer.

Pillar of Light or Basic Auric Shield

This is a classic shielding technique, one that every magician or psi-talented person should be familiar with. It's based on work that occurred in magical and psi circles at the early part of the 20th century.

Begin the following exercise by running through the basic grounding and centering exercises given above.

1. Once you have both grounded and centered, visualize/feel a glowing sphere of steel blue light glowing and spinning above your crown. It is cosmic force, creative/destructive primal energy, Divine essence.
2. Allow that shower of steel blue energy to flow down around you. It washes over your aura and completely seals you in a protective sphere of power. Regardless of what color you see your aura as being, this shields it within a force field of steel-blue energy. This force field should extend three or four feet above and below you and at least two feet in diameter around you.
3. Once you have this field securely set, visualize the interior being flooded with protective white light, light that washes away any stagnant or inhospitable energy.
4. Try to continue to feel or visualize this for at least five minutes.
5. Finally, visualize a personal symbol of power—it can be anything: a pentacle, cross, valknot, hammer—radiating on the force field at about the solar plexus area. This seals and locks the shield into place.
6. Then go ahead and let it fade from consciousness. It will still be there, though I recommend doing this exercise several times a day.

This is based on a "Pillar of Light" exercise given by Denning and Phillips in their book *The Art of Psychic Self Defense,* though again you will find variations cropping up throughout the occult community. It teaches you to construct a basic personal shield. Once you have mastered this technique, you can begin to experiment and adapt this shield to your needs and preferences. There is one caveat: as always, you must be adequately centered and grounded to shield effectively.

Shielding is many-faceted. Shields can be latent, set to activate only when incoming threat is detected; they can be active, always up and ready; they can include traps to capture and drain energy, tag the sender, etc.; they can be purely defensive or include offensive weaponry that will strike at anyone sending hostile energy. Ideally, a good shield matrix is a combination of all of these things.

Whenever possible, it is good to draw the imagery one uses to create a shield from nature. The closer to a natural pattern something is, the fewer ripples it makes on the fabric of being, the less it stands out, the less energy it takes and the more difficult it is for an enemy to locate. A good example would be a mountain shield that treats incoming hostile energy as wind. If the wind hits the mountain, it doesn't move the mountain. The mountain splits the wind, dispersing it to either side. This is an example of what Clan Tashlin (a family of magician-colleagues that I work with) calls "pattern magic": magic drawn from naturally occurring patterns found in nature. The goal here is to be as effective as possible while wasting as little energy as possible and, more importantly, attracting as little attention as possible.

Shields for Mediums

Mediums, as noted in the chapter on gifts, often have etheric/astral bodies that are not strongly connected to their physical bodies. This makes it easy for entities to come in. While this can be a useful gift when it's controlled, uncontrolled it can drive the medium to mental breakdown. This can be a difficult gift to shield, particularly if the medium isn't under the protection of a specific Deity.

First, ground and center as though your life depends upon it. More even than with empaths, this combination of exercises is necessary for a medium.

Second, if it is possible, call regularly upon your ancestors. Set up an ancestral altar and work with it regularly. Put pictures, objects that belonged to your dead, a copy of your genealogy, anything that reminds you of them, on the altar. Light candles, burn incense, offer fresh water and, on special occasions, food and wine to your dead. Talk to them, make them a part of your family, tell them what's occurring in your life as them to watch over you. This in and of itself can provide powerful protection to an untrained medium. Before anything else, I would encourage a medium to get his or her ancestral house in order. You don't need to know their names to call upon them. They know you. And if you're adopted, you have two sets of ancestors you can call upon: your birth ancestors and your adopted ones. Take advantage of this!

Third, shield the gift channel in addition to setting up a mental shield and magical shield. Most mediums, when they interact with spirits, can usually feel a place at the back or top of the head (or in some cases the heart chakra or soles of the feet) where the spirit will attempt to enter their body. This is the port to shield. This special shielding should be an integral part of any mental shield. After this, raise a good solid shield matrix. This doesn't have to be complex (and this holds true for anyone) but should include two, maybe three strong layers.

Camouflaging

There are a number of reasons to camouflage a shield. It can attract unwanted, annoying or even dangerous attention from discarnate entities, elementals, and other magicians. It's a walking advertisement that here is a person possessing power.

It can make those around you uncomfortable, even those who are mostly ungifted (and most people have at least a touch of a gift, even if only latent). It can feel as though you are blocking them or pushing them away (which you are, just not in the way their unconscious minds will register it). Those with the Sight will be able to see a shield and even take from its construction a measure of your power and skill. This is to be avoided from a tactical standpoint.

Chameleon Shields

Call the energy up around you just like you would with a bubble shield, but set its inherent pattern to reflect wherever it is you are. Tell it that it's chameleon skin. It should pick up the frequency of wherever it is you walk, and take that on itself. In essence, the external skin of the shield becomes like a moving picture screen, playing an image of whatever and wherever you happen to be walking. A similar effect can be achieved by setting the shield to be faceted like dozens of reflective prisms.

The downside of this is that if someone looks at you with the Sight, you won't appear to be there. There are some people who have an inborn talent for shielding and who *might* manage to shield this well without any training at all, but they are extremely rare.

Notice-Me-Nots

There are a couple of ways to cast this type of shield, but it works best with a bit of projective empathy. You create the image of how you want to be seen in your mind. Imbue it with emotion, projective empathic force that reinforces the image you wish to create (i.e.: "Nothing to see here") and then project it around yourself. You want to make people's eyes glance over and off of you. They literally will not see you. The shield should be set to 'broadcast' the "nothing interesting here" feeling, the "notice-me-not" and/or whatever image it is you wish to present.

If you're very, very gifted, you can set this shield, which, like any camouflage shield should be your outermost one, to reflect the energy field of a "normal" un-gifted person. This is a delicate thing, though, and I've always found it difficult to maintain. Keep in mind that this type of shield may waver or give with strong emotions. That is because it's more than a shield; you're actively affecting the mind of those people who may encounter you. It's a combination of telepathic and empathic suggestion carried in part by the energy raised for the shield itself.

Another useful notice-me-not provides us with a good example of "pattern magic" at work. Create a simple energy shield, just like you would for a bubble or mirror shield. Tell the shield that it is a rock and that all incoming emotions, energy and even people are water, water rushing in the stream in which the rock is situated. Set this shield to extend a bit more than normal from your aura. The "water" will hit the "rock" and part before it, just like real water would before a large rock in a rushing stream. This is a good shield to create and keep latent, hidden in your shield matrix or even your ground. Just tuck it away. You can consciously make it active when you are in large crowds or feeling particularly battered empathically.

A Note On Layering Shields

A good shield matrix is comprised of at least two or three layers. It's important to make sure that the layers are complementary and that they work well together. I would not, for instance, layer fire and wind shields one right over the other for the simple reason that fire tends to feed upon wind and there is too great a chance that these two shields would merge into one, thus defeating the purpose of layering. Give serious thought to how the various layers will interact. What will each layer do to incoming energy? This can tell you which order will be most favorable and effective.

When you're first learning how to shield, raise one good, solid shield and work with that for awhile. When you're comfortable with that, when it can go a day without being checked, then add a second layer. Work with the two of them for awhile until you're absolutely comfortable with them and until they remain strong and integrated. Then add a third. Don't rush this. It's better to take a bit of time, than to have weak or unstable shields.

Finally, as with anything else, the key to good shields is practice. Using one's psi-gifts and working actively with energy is very much like building up a muscle. It takes time and consistent, repetitive practice. So be patient with yourself and don't shirk on the practice part.

Warding

My work is an eclectic blend of various styles from hoodoo to pure energy work, pure psionics to ceremonial magic, with a healthy dose of clerical magic thrown in for good measure, and nowhere is this more strongly reflected than in how I ward a house. This largely stems from the fact that I'm a troubleshooter and extremely pragmatic. If it works, I'll use it. So the techniques that I suggest using when warding a house are equal parts ceremonial, hoodoo, and plain old nasty folk magic— and if you think witch's bottles aren't nasty, read the recipe below! I incorporate a great number of talismans and charms in warding a house for one reason and one reason alone: they are effective. Stones and herbs have their own energy. If I can accomplish up to a third of my house warding by using the inherent energies of these things, than that's a substantial amount of energy I myself do not have to lay out. This is all to the good. It's economical and efficient.

After setting up your personal shields, the next most important thing to do is to establish house wards. This does for your home what shielding does for you personally. They are really no more difficult to build and maintain than personal shields, and that's something to keep in mind as we go over these techniques. The benefit of house wards is that so much of it can be done with talismans; also, since they are restricted to one place, they tend to require less energy to maintain their strength.

Firstly, clean your house physically. Clutter collects stagnant and sometimes even negative energy. Clean your house and every time you go to reinforce your house wards, which should be at least once a month, you should begin by cleaning your house physically. This cleaning should be done as a gift to the home itself. Ideally, you don't just want to ward out negative and harmful energies. You want to bring peace and harmony into your home as well. Magic, like nature after all, abhors a vacuum.

Secondly, make an offering to your house spirits. In Norse tradition these are called *vaettir*, which is an all-purpose term for pretty much any unseen spirit that's not a ghost. *Vaettir* are intimately connected to the elements, to the energies of a home, to certain places and to certain organic things. They're somewhat analogous to the Japanese *kami*. Being on friendly terms with your house spirits can go a long way toward keeping the energy of a house clean and harmonious and well-balanced. I suggest setting aside a special bowl that is only used for *vaettir* offerings (they usually like alcohol, or milk and bread, or milk and honey—those are the traditional offerings anyway but you may get a strong feeling to offer something else and if you do, go with that feeling) and making regular weekly offerings. You can even ask them to help you keep the house pleasant and free of malignant energies.

Thirdly, clean your house magically. There are numerous ways to do this and many of them will be covered in the next chapter on cleansings. I would suggest using a combination of at least two in order to thoroughly magically cleanse your house. If you are a priest/ess or other clergy, or if you know a clergyperson of a compatible faith to your own, it doesn't hurt to have him or her come in and bless your home; if you can do it yourself, all the better. You can combine it with the house warding. When I ward my space, I often also bless and consecrate it. There are negative beings that will be deterred by the blessing.

One thing to watch out for: when you are cleaning your house magically, have a window cracked or leave the door open. You want to drive stagnant and/or negative energy out and it's important to give it somewhere to go. There is no "away". Energy doesn't just go away. It has to have somewhere to go.

Next, once your home has been thoroughly cleaned both magically and physically, you want to cast a ward around your home just like you would around yourself. It's very important to give this shield, which comprises the primary ward on your home, an external power source. I also suggest giving it a physical focus in the house itself. Let's look at how this is done.

Magically Warding The Home: The Energy Ward

First, select a focus. One common focus might be a stone that you resonate with, or a bottle or earth or seawater. I use a piece of tiger's eye (my preferred stone, one that I like and resonate very strongly with) the size of my head as the temporal and physical focus for my house wards. I placed this in a nook in a fairly central spot in my apartment. In every room, there is a smaller piece of tiger's eye, usually concealed to hook into and bolster the charm. I work well with stones, particularly with tiger's eye, hence why I chose a stone as the focal point of my work. They're stable, solid and hold energy very, very well.

I send down mental tendrils to wherever I want to draw the energy from. I personally draw my house wards from several of the nine worlds, worlds from which I have permission to draw. You will have to select accessible power sources. There is nothing wrong with drawing from the earth's core itself. If your dwelling sits on a ley line, it may be tempting to tie your shields into it, but this source of power can become rapidly depleted, which isn't good for you or the land.

Once I have my power source, I mentally tie those tendrils into my focus object so that energy rushes in and builds within the object itself. Then I start to thread that energy out around the perimeter of my house as well as the ceilings and floors (like a personal shield, a house ward must encompass all directions) using the smaller focal objects to lock the energy into its desired shape. As I do this, I tell the energy strongly what type of shield it will be, what it is set to be defending against, and how it should react. I also tell it where it will continue to draw its power from. After this, I make sure that the energy is A) feeding into the main focus object strongly and evenly and B) feeding into the ward itself equally strongly and evenly. It's important that there not be any holes or weak spots. Then I seal it both with a symbol of power (this too is a personal thing, a matter of inclination and choice) and a drop of my own blood drawn with a diabetic lancet.

If I intend to use more than one layer, I repeat this process and then consciously integrate the layers, making sure every layer is compatible with the next. I also tell my shields what type of energy they can feed upon in addition to their power source: storms, incoming attacks, ambient emotions from the building (I live in an apartment), etc.

If you don't want to use a physical focus, one could just as easily tie the ward into the electrical lines within one's apartment. I live in an old building, though, and I am a bit paranoid about putting any added stress on the wiring. You could also run the energy shield through the plumbing; pipes are perfectly shaped to be utilized as conduits for energy as well.

This is your basic and most fundamental house ward. You do almost exactly what you would do for a personal shield, save that a house ward is tied more strongly into a stationary power source.

Herbs, Camphor and Vinegar

I also suggest putting a camphor square in every corner of your bedroom. Camphor is a powerful substance and will block a great deal of spirit manifestation. Do not do this in the room that holds your ancestral altar—it can be unpleasant for them. You will have to change the camphor squares monthly as they do evaporate. If you can't find camphor squares, go ahead and use moth balls. Small cups of red vinegar in each room of your house will prevent negative spirit manifestation. I recommend changing the cups of vinegar every week.

Once you have done all of this, make a strong infusion of marjoram and basil. This is done by pouring boiling water over a tablespoon of each of the herbs and allowing it to steep for 20 minutes. Strain the herbs out and take that tincture clockwise around your house, asperging the ceiling, walls and floor. Basil and marjoram are happy herbs and will create feelings of harmony and contentment when used in this way. Basil also has some mild protective qualities.

Once you've done all of this, it's time to attack two of the weakest spots in any house: the threshold and all primary reflective surfaces (windows and mirrors). A threshold is a weak spot because so many people are constantly crossing it, bringing with them disparate and often undisciplined energies. Windows and mirrors are dangerous by their very nature as they can serve as doorways to the right type of being and also for magic. Fortunately, both are fairly easy to ward.

Warding The Threshold

There are a number of steps to properly warding a threshold.

1. Hang something of cold iron over your door; I use an old horseshoe. Their propensity for bringing good luck stems more from the cold iron for warding off certain kinds of energy than it does from the shape of the iron itself.
2. Hang a blessing charm (recipe below) over the door. I actually have numerous charms hanging over my door, each with its own specific function. Don't feel the need to limit yourself here.
3. Mix red ochre, dragonsblood and a few drops of your own blood and enough water to make a paste and paint the following protective sigils on your door. If you are Wiccan or generic Pagan, go ahead and use a pentacle or whatever other protective symbols you prefer; if you are comfortable with Northern Tradition symbols, use an *aegishjalmer* and down either side of the door the following runes: Teiwaz, Algiz, Othila. (For information on Norse or Saxon runes, and for the figure of the *aegishjalmer*/Helm of awe, see the Appendix.)
4. Take a length of chain. Affix nails and pins to it. Call upon the warrior God of your choice to bless and charge the chain, imbuing it with protective power. Really charge the hell out of it. Take a cigar and inhale the smoke blowing it out upon the chain several times. Take a mouthful of rum and spit it out on the chain to "feed" the chain. Do this several times. Hang this chain over the lintel of your front door (inside). This is a Lukumi protection charm that I learned from a Santero friend of mine. I call upon Heimdall, asking Him to guard my threshold when I do this. Originally the charm is meant to call upon Ogoun. I suggest adapting it for whatever warrior Deity you most resonate with.

5. Hang small knives on either side of your door. They should be charged to cut any offensive, harmful, malignant incoming energy.

6. Regularly sprinkle the door and the threshold itself with blessed water or water with a few drops of protective oil blended in.

7. Keep salt regularly sprinkled across your threshold (outside the door).

8. Regularly do the Pentacle Warding Charm (given below) on the door from the inside of your house.

9. When you are having people over, particularly if you don't know them very well, put a big bowl of water behind the door, or as near to the door as you can. It will absorb negative energy as people come through the door.

You will have to "feed" these wards regularly. This is done by asperging with cigar smoke or rum. Every couple of months, I recommend repainting the sigils. The Pentacle Warding should be repeated at least monthly, if not weekly.

Like any other shield, you will want to camouflage your house and threshold wards. This can be done one of two ways: you can cast another external energy ward designed to conceal the others or, if you have facility at working with *wyrd* (which will be discussed in the chapter at the end of the book), you can grab the fabric of the *wyrd*-plane and pull it over you. This is much like wrapping yourself in the fabric of night and will render you invisible. The same type of camouflage shields, particularly the prism shield, described above in the section on personal shields, will also work very well for concealing a house ward. More so even than personal shields, it's important for safety's sake, that the house wards look as unprepossessing as possible.

Warding Windows and Mirrors

Unwarded windows and mirrors make excellent doorways and can provide entry points for unwanted negative magic. Therefore it's of utmost importance that both be strongly warded when securing your home. I do this by way of the warding charms given below.

Pentacle Warding Charm

The first and strongest charm that I know is one I learned roughly fifteen years ago from my first teacher. It is very ceremonial and I have adapted it for my own usage as I am a hard polytheist and the original all-encompassing "Goddess and God" attributions didn't sit well with me (my adaptation is given below in brackets beside the original). Choose an oil that you like. I usually use whatever I have at hand, though there are numerous protective oils. A good dragon's blood oil would be perfect for this. Raise energy, drawing it into your hands and imbuing or charging the oil with that energy.

Pour some of the oil onto your fingers. Starting at the lower left corner, draw a line to the top center point saying "By the Name that is above all Names, by the Great Goddess and Her Mighty Lord (or insert the names of a God and Goddess that you prefer)."

Draw from the center point to the lower right corner saying: "I banish all influences and seeds of evil."

Draw from the lower right corner to the upper left corner: "I lay upon them a spell of holiness and power..."

Draw from top left corner across to top right: "That they be bound fast as with chains..."

Draw from the top right corner to the lower left corner: "And cast into the outer darkness..."

Touch the center of the pentacle: "That they trouble not this servant of the Gods."

Do this on your door and on every window and mirror in your house. Then, using the same oil, draw either the rune Algiz or the rune Ior on the windows, mirrors and doors. Next, I hang a blessing charm over each window and over the door. I do not hang such a charm over the mirrors, though one could, if they were special cause for concern.

Blessing Charm

This charm is for peace, harmony, and protection within the home. In a green pouch, combine the following ingredients:

3 pinches of basil (protection)
1 large pinch of marjoram (harmony and peace)
1 cross stone (grounding and stability)
1 small jalap root (power)
1 tonka bean (pleasant relationships and luck)
1 garnet (very protective)
1 black tourmaline (excellent for absorbing and shunting negative energy away)
A piece of turquoise (to ward off evil)
Three runes, if you work with them: Teiwaz, Algiz, Othila. Their names should be chanted and they should be anointed with the ochre/dragon's blood/blood mixture that I note above. If you are not comfortable with Norse symbols, use the protective sigil of your choice.

Charge it strongly, imprinting it with the idea of peace and harmony. Draw the power symbol of your choice over the bag to seal it. Hang them up and do not open them. Opening them will disperse the magic.

This is the recipe that I use most often, but there is no need to feel that you must limit yourself to this particular charm. There are a number of good books on the market listing the magical properties of plants, herbs, roots and stones. Personally, I highly recommend Catherine Yronwode's *Hoodoo Herb and Root Magic*. Once you have a good compendium, you can make your own talismans. The idea is to combine ingredients of compatible energies so that the combined whole produces a desired effect. I encourage experimentation here.

Witch's Bottles

Once you've done everything else listed above, make a witch's bottle. I love witch's bottles, I really do. They're nasty, easy to make, and very effective. Witch's bottles date back at least to the early 18th century (they've been found buried in the foundations of houses from this period in both England and the United States) and are charms designed to absorb and disperse negative, malignant, and harmful energies. The power is derived from the combination of ingredients.

Get a good sturdy mason jar. Once this thing is sealed you do *not*, under any circumstances, want to open it again. In the jar combine as many of the following ingredients as you can come up with:

Nine rusty nails	Rue
Bent pins	Dragon's blood
House dust	Jalap
Tangled bits of string	Red and black pepper
Broken glass	Cayenne pepper
Broken mirror	Thorns (especially whitethorn or
Old razor blades	blackthorn)
Barbed wire	Any other baneful herbs available
Small fishing hooks	

Now urinate in the bottle. This is an absolute necessary part of the spell. As noted in a previous charm above, you're essentially pissing on your enemies and marking your territory. Add enough water to fill the jar and seal it securely. Pour black candle wax over the top of the jar and around its mouth sealing it securely.

There are two ways to dispose of a witch's bottle, and I prefer the second. The first is to bury it outside, and the second is to hide it in your house somewhere where you won't have to see it regularly. I stuck mine way back in the corner of my bathroom behind a cabinet. Once this is made, put it away and leave it alone. Don't think about it again. Trust it to do its job.

Window Bottles

I like to think of this as a modified witch's bottle. These are prettier than your average witch's bottle and are good to hang in windows. They'll trap and disperse any incoming negative energy. Acquire a couple of pretty bottles in various colors. Flea markets, yard sales, antique stores are all good places to look. Put the following ingredients in the jar: A thin coil of copper wire, tangled red thread, and bent pins. Fill with water and seal.

I've known some who just use the thread and the copper. Some people add house dust to this, some add baneful herbs, some urinate in the bottle. I've found all variation on this to be equally effective. Again, you do not want to open these bottles once they've been sealed. In the event that one explodes, it means it has taken a powerful incoming attack for you and you may want to increase and strengthen your house wards and take the necessary steps to ward off attack. Once these are constructed, hang them in your windows.

War Water

This is not something that I suggest using regularly. It's a very intense spell and can feel very hot and heavy within a home. This is something to use when you feel yourself to be under magical attack. War water is a floor-wash. You're actually going to be washing any hard wood or linoleum floors in your house, the threshold of your door, your front steps, and anywhere else you think necessary with this mixture.

Take a bucket of water and add a cup of ammonia. Blend the following ingredients in a large jar, and add one cup of the mixture to the bucket of water and ammonia.

Pinch of salt
1 teaspoon saltpeter
Pinch of black pepper
1-2 tablespoons of cayenne

9 rusty nails
1 piece of jalap root
Handful of crushed mint
3 pinches of dragon's blood
Urine
Add enough water to top off the jar.

I recommend making this up and keeping it in a jar, and then adding a cup as needed to the ammonia and water blend. Urine is essential: you are again symbolically pissing on your enemies and establishing dominance while at the same time marking your space. If you don't have access to jalap or saltpeter, don't worry about it. Add more peppers or other abrasive spices. Substitution is ok. If you don't have rusty nails, don't worry about it. Use regular nails. They'll rust soon enough.

Uncrossing Charm

This is something I like to do every new moon. It is a traditional uncrossing charm, which will banish a good deal of low level negative energy sent your way.

Ingredients: A large grey candle, preferably one that can be removed from its glass. This is what's called a seven-day (or *novena*, meaning nine-day) candle. A nail to carve the sigil into the candle, a lancet, and some dragon's blood powder. If the candle can't be removed from the jar, use a marker for drawing on the glass.

Carve the sigil (given in the Appendix) on the candle or draw it with the marker on the glass. It is better to do this directly on the candle, so try your best to find the type of seven-day candles that can be removed from the glass, or use a large candle that doesn't have glass. On the back, if you like, you can carve your name and astrological sign. If you have a personal sigil (some magicians do), use that instead.

Prick your finger with the lancet and put a few drops of your own blood in the center of the sigil. Rub the carvings with dragon's blood powder. Rub the wick as well with dragon's blood powder for good measure.

Charge the candle, holding it between your hands and filling it with energy. (Candle magic will be discussed in depth in the section on energy work.) When you feel the candle can take no more, seal the energy in by tracing the sigil of your choice over it. I was taught to use a pentacle. Light the candle and allow it to burn down fully. If the candle is in a glass holder, you can put the whole thing in a metal pot of water when you're not in the house. That way, if the glass cracks, the water will put out the flame.

There are also a number of magical cleansing rituals which are very useful to know; most notably the Hammer Hallowing and the Lesser Banishing Ritual of the Pentagram.

Hammer Hallowing

This rite has fallen out of favor in modern Heathenry over the past few years, largely because it is not historically based. It was, I believe, invented in the 20th century by Edred Thorsson, himself a ceremonial magician. Regardless of its historical accuracy or lack thereof, it's incredibly powerful when performed rightly. Again, this should be chanted or sung, the power coming in large part through the power of one's voice. This is called *galdr* and is a very powerful form of Northern Tradition magic. It doesn't matter if you have a nice voice or not. *Galdr* comes from the old Norse word *gala*, which means "to croak" or "to caw". If you do not have the resources to learn to pronounce the Old Norse, use the English translations.

Ideally, you should have a small sledge hammer, one that can be easily held in the hand and swung. A consecrated knife works just as well. If you have neither, simply use your hand to make the hammer symbol, which is a vertical line drawn from top to bottom, with a horizontal line across the bottom; the symbol of Thor's hammer, sort of like an upside-down capital T.

Begin by standing in the North. With the hammer, knife or even your hand extended in front of you, beginning chanting each of the runes in order, drawing them in front of you as you do so. While you do this, you should be moving in a clockwise circle to the right, so that at the end of your runic recitation, the runes completely encompass you in that circle of protection.

Standing in the North again, make the sign of the hammer while chanting: *Hamarr í Norðri helga vé þetta ok hald vörð!* (*Hammer in the North hallow and hold this holy stead* or, more literally according to Thorsson: *Hammer in the North hallow this sacred enclosure and keep watch over it.*)

Turn east and again make the sign of the hammer intoning: *Hamarr í Austri helga vé þetta ok hald vörð!* (*Hammer in the east, Hallow and hold this holy stead.*)

Turn south and make the sign of the hammer intoning: *Hamarr í Suðri helga vé þetta ok hald vörð!* (*Hammer in the South, hallow and hold this holy stead.*)

Turn West and make the sign of the hammer and intone: *Hamarr í Vestri helga vé þetta ok hald vörð!* (*Hammer in the West, hallow and hold this holy stead.*)

Standing again in the North, make the hammer sign overhead intoning: *Hamarr yfir mér helga vé þetta ok hald vörð!* (*Hammer over me hallow and hold this holy stead.*)

Do the same below you into the floor: *Hamarr undir mér helga vé þetta ok hald vörð!* (*Hammer under me hallow and hold this holy stead.*)

Now extend your arms to either side in a cross and intone: *Hamarr Helga vé þetta ok hald vörð!* (*Hammer hallow and hold this holy stead.*)

Do this once in each of the other four directions and once for the vertical axis. Finally, stand in the center of the newly warded space, make one final hammer sign and touch the hammer to the floor. As you make the hammer sign, intone: *Um mik ok í mér Àsgarðr ok Miðgarðr!* (*Around me and in me Asgard and Midgard.*)

(This is my adaptation of the hammer rite as given in *Futhark: A Handbook of Rune Magic* by Edred Thorsson, published by Samuel Weiser, Inc., ME: 1984, p. 91-92.)

Weonde Song

This was developed by Swain Wodening and the Ealdriht, a group of Anglo-Saxon Heathens, as a means of hallowing space prior to their rituals. I do this while fire dancing with hand lamps, using the fire to cleanse not only places but, if needed, specific things as well. This can be easily done by carrying a candle around one's house, or a torch around one's external dwelling. The Old English translates roughly as:

Fire I bear around this sacred enclosure
Bringing peace and holiness.
I bid all ill wishing spirits away.
Thor make sacred
Thor make sacred
Thor make sacred this holy place.

The second stanza is the same, save that it bids all outlaws to be away. This charm should be sung and the power for magic comes partly through the fire itself and partly through the voice. Channel the power you raise through the song itself.

Fyr ic bere ymb friðgearde,
Ond béode men frið fremman,
Líeg ic bere tó belùcan,
Béode aelwihta fléogan aweg.
Thunor wéoh,
Thunor wéoh,
Thunor wéohþisne ealh.

Fyr ic bere ymb friðgearde,
Ond béode men frið fremman,

Líeg ic bere tó belùcan,
Béode utlaga féran aweg.
Thunor wéoh,
Thunor wéoh,
Thunor wéohþisne ealh.
Thunor wéoh,
Thunor wéoh,
Thunor wéohþisne ealh.

The Lesser Banishing Ritual of the Pentagram (LBRP)

This is a Kabbalistic rite common to certain branches of ceremonial magic. It was one of the first protection rituals that I learned and remains a potent tool in my arsenal. If you're uncomfortable invoking the Hebraic names and Deity, then don't use this. I'm including the version I learned here for authenticity. It invokes four different names of the Hebraic God, and the four archangels. I also believe this should be sung or chanted for maximum power.

Begin with the Kabbalistic Cross: Standing facing east, center yourself. Extend your right hand out in front of you above your forehead palm up. Draw power into your hand. See/Feel it gathering there in a glowing, golden sphere. Bring that power in and touch your forehead intoning *Atah (to You be).*

Touch your breastbone intoning: *Malkuth (the Kingdom).*

Touch your right shoulder intoning: *Ve Geburah (the Power).*

Touch your left shoulder intoning: *Ve Gedulah (the Glory).*

Cross your arms over your chest intoning: *Le Olahm, Amen. (for ever and ever, so be it).*

This is the Kabbalistic Cross. It seals the aura. Next, draw the pentagrams. Standing in the east again, starting at the lower left corner and drawing up to the middle point, draw a five pointed star. I actually go from floor to as high as I can reach when I do this. Then point to the center of the star and intone the sacred name: *Yod He Vod He.*

Turn south and make the same pentagram intoning: *Adonai.*

Turn west and make the pentagram intoning: *Eheieh.*

Turn North and make the pentagram intoning: *Agla.*

(The first three are Divine names and the last is a contraction of a Hebraic phrase that means *"thou art mighty forever, oh Lord."*)

As you draw the pentagrams, see the energy glowing in the air. Next, turn east again and call upon the Archangels: Extend your arms out in a cross and intone/chant:

Before me stands Raphael
Behind me stands Gabriel
On my right hand stands Michael
On my left hand stands Uriel
Above and below me shine the six pointed star
And around me flame the pentacles.
May their light now descend.
May the power of the holy Shekinah descend.

Repeat the drawing of the pentagrams and intoning of sacred names from East to North. Close with the Kabbalistic Cross.

When one is just starting out, it's a good idea to do some sort of protective rite, either the hammer or the LBRP every night. The protective power of these rituals, when done with proper focus, will accrue, building up a reservoir in your home. This is an advantage in working any type of cleansing or protective magic.

Warding Your Vehicle

Just as you ward your house, you also need to ward your vehicle. In fact, I would say it's even more important to have good protections on a car than it is on a house because there is more of a chance of an accident while driving.

The easiest way to do this is to cast an energy shield exactly the same way that you would on your home, save that the power for the shield comes from the car engine itself. Every time you rev the engine, the shield is fed more power.

You may, in addition to this shield (*not* instead of), call upon the God or Goddess of your choice (I usually prefer Gna, the messenger Goddess of the Norse and/or Thor, Protector of Midgard) to empower the following charm, then charge the hell out of it.

Another method is to use a piece of horse's tail braided around a metal ring. Affix to this a small pouch of comfrey and a small tiger's eye. You can anoint this with blood, or protective oil.

Cleansing

Cleanliness is next to godliness, and had better come first.
-Aleister Crowley

There is an old saying: "An ounce of prevention is worth a pound of cure." There is much wisdom in this saying and it holds doubly true for magic. When I was first learning how to practice magic, I spent a solid year doing almost nothing but cleansing rituals alone. I thought I was the cleanest apprentice in the tri-state area! I realize now, years later the wisdom and pragmatism of my teacher in forcing me to focus on something so seemingly insignificant as cleansing. Knowing how to clean your house and your person magically and doing so in a regular basis *whether or not you feel you are under attack* is one of the best and most essential things you can do by way of psychic hygiene. This holds true not only for magicians, but for psi-talented folks and for anyone who practices ritual work – in fact, for anyone at all. It's a wonderful panacea not only for magical nastiness but for general malaise and stress as well.

In this chapter, you will receive the basics of magical cleansing for people, places, and things. There is much more to cleansing than what could be written in any book, but the material here will provide you with a good grounding in these techniques which, if practiced with regularity, will do much to provide adequate protection (as well as to reduce stress, which after all, is unfocused negative energy).

The first round of defense in the war against magical grime and malignancy is to physically clean your house. As noted previously, clutter attracts stagnant energy. It's only one step further for that to become a breeding ground for negative energy. Before anything else, clean your house thoroughly on a physical level.

Next comes the cleansing bath. The cleansing bath utilizes various combinations of substances in much the same way creating a magical charm bag does. The combination of energies from the ingredients creates a desired outcome, in this case, the removal of negative energies. There are two ways to take a cleansing bath: the traditional way and the comfortable way. Traditionally, one made the requisite infusion and let it sit and steep straining it into a jar when cool. Then one stripped down, stood in the tub or shower and poured the infusion over one's head and body. Then, without drying off (it is considered important in some traditions not to wipe the infusion off) allow yourself to air dry and dress in clean clothes. If the infusions are warm, this isn't so bad, but generally they're stone cold, which is unpleasant.

The more comfortable way of taking a cleansing bath, and the one I personally prefer, is to add a cup or two of the requisite infusion to the bath water itself and to soak. Magic demands enough sacrifices; why suffer when you don't have to? It's good to have two ways though, because if you live in an apartment with only a shower, you have an option.

Below, I offer a few common types of cleansing baths. Please don't limit yourself to my recipes alone. Acquire a good magical herbal, or better yet, I highly recommend Catherine Yronwode's hoodoo and rootwork course available at www.luckymojo.com. Hoodoo stresses cleansing baths almost as much as my first teacher did! For the record, any combination of cleansing and purification herbs can be used in cleansing bath. (It is also possible to create baths to bring luck, abundance, and happiness into your life, but that is a bit beyond the magical scope of this book). I recommend taking at least one cleansing bath *per week*. There have been times in my magical life where the first thing I did upon coming home every single day was to take a cleansing bath. You cannot employ this particular activity too often.

Beer Bath

My favorite cleansing bath, and one that I try to do at least twice a month, is a German folk custom called the beer bath. I was dubious at first about this one, I'll admit, but it's one of the single most effective cleansing bath recipes that I have ever tried, and I've tried a lot of recipes. To use this bath, add a large bottle of dark beer to your bath water. Soak for at least ten minutes, being sure to douse every part of your body, including the crown of your head. The water disperses the smell of the beer, so don't worry about the smell, it's negligible. If you like, you can add a handful of kosher or sea salt to the bath water, but this isn't strictly necessary.

Vinegar and Salt Bath

The very first cleansing bath recipe that I ever learned was an equally simple one: one cup of apple cider vinegar and a half cup of salt added to the bath water. Again, soak for at least ten minutes and be sure to douse everything including your head.

If you have nothing else at hand, a cup of salt will do a pretty good job, particularly if you consecrate it first. Hold your hand over the salt and say something to the effect of "I bless and consecrate you, oh creature of earth, that you may cleanse and purify driving out all malignancy. So mote it be." Words have immense power in magic, and the simple act of consecration can work wonders.

Very Basic Cleansing Bath

In two quarts of apple cider vinegar add 2 tablespoons of each of the following: lavender, rosemary, sage, wormwood, mint, and rue. Add six mashed cloves of garlic. Let sit for 6 weeks in a cool, dark place. Add a bit of crumbled camphor. This will keep for several months. Strain out a cup and add to your bath when you wish to take a cleansing bath.

Another Basic Cleansing Bath

Make a strong infusion of the following herbs: peppermint, fennel, rue, chervil, and mugwort. Add the infusion to your bath along with a cup of kosher or sea salt.

Very Basic White Bath

Take seven carnations and as you bathe, scrub yourself down with the flowers. This will cleanse the aura.

Traditional White Bath

In Afro-Caribbean traditions, white baths are associated with Obatala, the orisha of cleanliness, purity, and order. His name means "King of the white cloth," which symbolizes serenity. White baths are often prescribed to cleanse and purify when practitioners are under stress or magical attack or for any other reason need serenity and clarity returned to their lives. Basically, you combine a number of white ingredients, white being Obatala's color. Certain purifying herbs are also added.

The recipe below may necessitate a trip to your local Botanica. This bath takes 8 days. You will need a white seven day candle in offering to Obatala.

Quita Maldicion	Milk from four coconuts
Almond leaves	Goat's milk
Cascarilla	Shea butter
Maravilla (Calendula)	Peppermint
White flowers	One coconut that is not part of the bath mixture.

The *Maldicion* (sacred beans used by Yoruba practitioners) must soak in water for at least one night. Shred it into cold water while praying to Obatala and your ancestors and allow this to steep overnight.

1. Mix all the non-flowering herbs into cold water and let sit. I recommend letting them soak in jars which you can cap. That way you can keep the mixture, easily adding what you need for the bath each night.
2. Sing to Obatala, pray to Him and ask His blessing, ask Him to lend His power to this bath.
3. Sing to your ancestors and ask them to lend their power and blessing as well.

4. Sprinkle the *cascarilla* and white flower petals over the bath right before use on the first of the eight days.

5. Refrigerate the goat's milk and coconut milk (and you must actually crack the coconuts and acquire the milk yourself; do not use canned milk) and add each day to the bath along with a cup of the herbal mixture.

6. Before bathing, light the candle in offering to Obatala. You will blow it out after your bath each day until the very last day.

7. While in the bath, rub yourself down with the herbs and leaves from that day's allotment of the mixture. Be sure to douse your head with the bath water.

8. Before the bath, dust a coconut with *cascarilla* chalk. After the bath, clean yourself with the coconut. Rub it all over yourself, cleansing your aura, all the while offering it to Obatala.

9. After the bath, discard the remaining leaves that may be in your tub into a river or ocean. It's disrespectful to just throw them in the garbage. If you don't have access to a large body of water, bury them in the ground.

10. On the eight day of the bath, let the candle burn out. Gather up all the used herbs in a white cloth. Tie it with a red ribbon. Take this bundle and the coconut to a white tree (either a birch or preferably a cotton tree) and leave it.

11. To thank Obatala for His blessings, some time after the bath, take two coconuts covered in *cascarilla* chalk and eight pennies in a bag (eight is His number) and put them under a white tree or in a bush. Make sure no one can see.

Calming Bath

3-5 sliced oranges
Cinnamon sticks
Whole cloves
White flowers
Honey

Collonia 1800 Sandalo (available at most Botanicas) or your favorite oil or cologne.

Let all of this steep for awhile in room temperature water. Warm it up but do not bring it to a boil. Add rum and while standing in a bath, pour the entire mixture over yourself from head down. Just bask in the scent.

Seven African Powers Cleansing Bath

Make a strong infusion of rosemary. Add seven capfuls of white rum. Light a candle to the Seven African Powers (the following orisha: Obatala, Ogun, Ellegua, Yemaya, Chango, Oshun, Oya).

Add this to your bath each night for seven days. As you bathe, keep the candle going. You may blow it out after each night except on the last day when it should be allowed to burn down completely. This is particularly good when your energy is being drained and also as a general clearing.

Sweet and Sour Bath

This bath breaks up negative influences and brings in positive ones. Make a strong infusion of the following herbs and add it to your bath:

To break up bad influences:
   Rue
   Poke root
   Salt
   Rosemary
   Ammonia (add last)
To bring good influences into your life:
   White flowers
   Honey
   Your favorite perfume
   Lavender

Seven Day Frigga Cleansing Bath

Frigga is the Goddess of the home in Norse cosmology. She is incredibly powerful in Her own right and is not to be underestimated. Boil one cup each of the following herbs for 20 minutes:

Rosemary
Fresh squeezed lime juice
Basil
Chamomile
Cinnamon
Lavender
Rose petals or lemon verbena

Ask Frigga's blessing as you boil the herbs. Ask that She banish any negativity or harmful energies being sent your way. Add a cup of the resulting infusion to your bath for seven days straight.

From these examples, I think you can get the general idea. The recipes are many and different but the desired result is the same. If you do nothing else, do not neglect weekly or at the very least monthly cleansing baths.

Another important source to call on for cleansing is the elements. Just as with shielding, it is possible to call upon the elements for cleansings of persons, places, and things.

Cleansing With Air

Air cleansings usually involve smoke or incense. One may burn a cigar and use the smoke to purify a room, an item or even a person. Tobacco makes a fine offering to spirits and ancestors and even some Deities. Burning *recels* (pronounced *ray-kels*), or bundles of herbs to cleanse is a practice attested to in surviving Anglo-Saxon medical manuals (and in those days, there was little difference between medicine and magic). The Celts called it *saining*. Today this is called smoking or smudging; the latter term came into Neo-Pagan traditions from Native American spiritual practices. The herbs are lit and the fire blown out so that the herbs burn slowly, emitting smoke. The smoke is then passed around whoever or whatever needs to be cleansed. Crushed herbs and resins can be burnt on small charcoals as well to achieve the same effect. Carrying this type of smoke throughout one's house is an excellent way to purify the dwelling. Some of the best herbs and resins to use for cleansing and purification are:

Dragon's blood (this is heavy duty)
Sage
Mugwort
Frankincense
Camphor
Eucalyptus
Hyssop
Rosemary
Copal
Lemon balm
Cedar
Tobacco
Garlic
Asafetida (Warning: this is absolutely vile! Some people are highly sensitive to this herb, so test it out before you burn it. I've known it to make some magicians vomit copiously. It is effective, though, and quite powerful.)

Serious Banishing Incense

Equal parts agrimony, rue and vervain plus ½ part dragon's blood.

Three Good Cleansing Incenses

These are not as strong as the above incense by any means; however, they're perfectly serviceable purifying blends nonetheless.

1. Equal parts sage, cinnamon and rosemary.
2. Frankincense, cinnamon, brown sugar.
3. Equal parts myrrh, white sandalwood, cedar, with one half part dragon's blood powder.

Purification Incense

Equal parts thoroughly ground: Frankincense, white sandalwood, copal.

One can also cleanse with sound, which is also associated magically with air. Sound vibrations have the ability to break up stagnant energies. Using a rattle in every room in your house or better yet, a Tibetan singing bowl, with the conscious intent of driving out negative or stagnant energy, is a potent cleansing method. Be sure to have a window open when you clean a house magically as the energy needs somewhere to go.

Tuning forks can be used to clear negative energy out of stones. This is extremely efficient because it takes no personal energy, nor does it require any innate psi or magical talent. I use a tuning fork with the frequency of C 4096 to clear stones of any negative energy and one charged to 156.1 Herz to infuse them with earth energies. The spirits of the stones absolutely love this. Both tuning forks can be purchased at www.biosonics.com.

I know of one magician who, before she moved into her new house, took a CD player and set it to repeat one CD over and over again, playing the Heart Sutra for a solid 48 hours before moving in. She said it left her new home cleansed and blessed like nothing else she'd ever done, so don't underestimate the use of sound and music in ritual cleansings.

Cleansing With Fire

Fire will happily feed upon all types of energy and has been used the world over in consecrating, blessing and cleansing rituals. Carrying a candle around your home, while chanting or singing the *Weonde* song found earlier in this section, is an excellent method of both blessing and consecrating your home. Better yet, bless and charge one candle for every room in your house. Allow that candle to burn down, having charged it with the instructions that as it burns, it will devour all negative energy. (Information on candle magic is provided in the chapter on energy work).

Remember that each of the elements is alive. They have their own type of sentience. They are deserving of respect. Furthermore, in many traditions, including my own Norse one, the elements are our eldest of ancestors, so be courteous and polite with them.

Cleansing With Water

In addition to cleansing baths, which certainly fall under the category of "cleansing with water", there are several other ways to utilize water for this purpose. Water can be extremely protective as well. A simple charm to protect while you sleep is to put a glass of water by your bed. Throw it away every morning, cleaning the glass thoroughly and don't use the glass for anything else.

Infusions of various herbs can also be sprinkled about one's home to cleanse and alter the energy in the house. A blend of marjoram and basil is particularly good for this. Certain colognes, which can be purchased in botanicas are also excellent for this purpose. My personal favorite is called *Sandalo*. This is also very effective at "cooling" a space down after magical workings.

Stones and other items can be cleansed by soaking them in salt water overnight. The water should then be flushed down the toilet.

Cleansing With Earth

There are a number of ways this element can be called upon in cleansings.

1. Crystals or other stones can be charged to collect negative energy, or incoming hostile energy and can then be placed at strategic points around one's home. The downside of this is that they will need to be cleansed regularly.
2. Items can be buried in the earth overnight for cleansing.
3. Sand, soil, *cascarilla* powder, even seeds can be charged to collect negative energy and then sprinkled over the floor of one's home. This is then swept up and out of the house.
4. Stalks of plants like mugwort, flowers, etc. can be used to actually rub a person down, cleansing them of negative energies.
5. Salt is a gift of the earth and is extraordinarily cleansing by itself. It may be sprinkled in a house and the vacuumed or swept up, added to baths or sprinkled across the threshold.

Housecleaning Method

One cleanses a house, a place or a person in much the same way: by utilizing a combination of these techniques. I recommend the following combination for a basic house cleaning:

1. Clean the house physically.
2. Smudge with one of the cleansing herbs mentioned above.
3. Carry fire through each room, asking that fire bless the space and remove any negative energy.
4. Asperge with an infusion of cleansing herbs.
5. Sprinkle salt over the threshold and the windowsills.

Head Cleanings

In some traditions, most notably the Afro-Caribbean, people are believed to have a guardian spirit of the head. This is essentially that part of us that is always in connection with Deity, our Higher Selves if you will. In times of stress, exhaustion, magical attack, it can be very helpful to 'feed' this spirit by performing a head cleansing. Various combinations of herbs can be used, and it is rather messy but very, very effective. I recommend doing this at least once a year. I offer a traditional Santerian head cleansing as it was taught to me years ago (I am an eclectic magic worker). I have also used various combinations of herbs and powders for this purpose with great effect. I offer one of my own combinations as well for comparison. Use your intuition here or seek out a qualified practitioner to prescribe a head cleaning.

Head Cleaning #1

Begin by giving an offering to Oshun, the Orisha of love, affection, fertility, relationships. She likes honey, oranges, eggs, or gold. For this cleansing you will need the following:

Coconut water
River water or rain water
Goats milk
Rice water (soak rise in a pot of water outside overnight)
Cocoa butter
White juice fruits like pineapples, pears, honey dew
    and sweet soursop

Mix these ingredients together and wash your head with them, consciously offering this head cleaning to the spirit of your head.

Head Cleaning #2

Begin by making an offering to Freya. She likes honey, honey powder, Goldschlager, expensive chocolate, amber, amber and more amber, gold, strawberries with honey, nice perfume, etc. Mix the following:

Honey

Crushed and powdered amber

Damiana

Rue

Milk (preferably sweetened condensed milk)

Goat's milk

Cinnamon

Ground coffee beans

Shea butter

Wash your head with this mixture consciously, offering it to the spirit of your head.

Magical Oils

There are numerous recipes on the market for magical oils, so I'm only going to offer a couple of my own recipes here. Oils can be used for blessing and consecrating, to mark one's ownership of an object, to draw protective sigils on people, places, and things. While one of the clearest and most powerful ways to mark ownership of an object or to mark a person as under your own protection is to mark with one's own blood, this isn't always appropriate. There are health concerns, especially when marking another person or an object which will be handled by others. Blood also creates the single strongest connection one can possibly have with an item. If that item is lost or falls into the wrong hands, the results could be most unpleasant. So, all in all, it's better to not generally use blood, hence the proliferation of magical oils. Most oils are mixed by adding a certain number of drops to a carrier oil; I prefer to use sweet almond oil.

Power and protection oil

Jalap, one small chunk

2 parts dragon's blood

1 part frankincense

½ part poke root
½ part galangal

Mix into a base oil of sweet almond oil and store with a piece of carnelian.

Power Oil

(This works as an incense too if one blends the required resins.)
Equal parts frankincense oil, myrrh and dragon's blood oils

Blessing Oil #1

1 part wisteria, 1 part rose, ½ part lavender

Blessing Oil #2

Equal parts benzoin, wisteria, and lilac

Purification Oil

1 part camphor
½ part musk
½ part rose
A touch of patchouli

Quick Fix Protection Rite

I'm going to close this chapter with a quick fix protection rite that I learned from my ceremonialist teacher. This is based on a medieval prayer, and apparently my teacher found it quoted in a novel, though she never told me the title of the book and we've since fallen out of touch. If anyone knows where this has been used, I would love to have the original source.

This does not provide long lasting protection. I wouldn't depend on it for more than twenty minutes, but that is ample time to clean a house or person. This is a nice protection ritual to do before going into a situation where you know you will be dealing with tainted, dangerous, or malignant energy. It does not substitute for good shields before, during and after, and cleansing work after the fact.

Stand and center yourself. Perform the Kabbalistic Cross. Extend your arms to the side and say with focused intent:

By the power of the Gods within me,
Whom I serve with all my heart, with all my soul, and with all my breath,

Begin turning in a clockwise circle saying:

I now encompass myself about in this circle of Divine protection
Across which no mortal or immortal error dares to set its foot.

Perform the Kabbalistic Cross to close the rite.

Magical Tools

I want to say a few words about magical tools. These are generally associated with Wicca, but they actually stem from Renaissance and later ceremonial magic. We see them represented in the Minor Arcana of the Tarot along with their elemental representations. Magicians work with the four classical elements: air, fire, water, and earth. Each element has a magical tool associated with it. These tools occasionally come in handy in magical workings, including protection work so I'm going to touch on them briefly here, though, with the exception of the knife, they do not figure greatly in my own work.

The Tool of Air: The Knife

Magically, air is usually associated with the intellect, with the power of decision making, with clarity, purification, cleansing, and cutting free of that which is no longer needed. It represents intellectual pursuits, fluency and facility with language – including the ability to cut someone to ribbons with words – and the power of speech as magical manifestation. The negative traits of this element are flightiness, lack of focus, and a certain vapidity. The traditional direction of this element is East, its colors are either blues and whites (or yellow, depending on which ceremonial tradition one practices), and its traditional tool is the knife.

To be honest, I've found that of all the tools, I only ever regularly use my knife (or *athame*). This is an all-purpose tool, consecrated and blessed, fully charged and ready to be used for combat or such practical needs as cutting bread or cutting thread.

Please keep your knife in good working order. I absolutely *deplore* the fallacy that has circulated in Pagan and some magical circles for years that one's working blade should be dull. This is an utter disgrace: to the magic, to the spirit of the blade itself, to the physical weapon and to every single one of your ancestors who had to use a blade for survival. All blades should be in good working order, oiled and sharpened at all times. This idea that blades should be dulled, that the edge should be actively and consciously blunted is, to be quite blunt, a load of New Age bullshit.

Please do *not* purchase a decorative blade. Purchase a real knife, one that could stand up to a bit of hard work. Either go to a sporting goods store and check out their selection of blades, or find a good online dealer: ragweedforge.com, knifeworks.com, or coldsteel.com are all excellent online shops with an extensive and well priced catalog. Learn how to care for your knife, including how to properly *sharpen* it. I prefer to have one fixed blade for fighting and magical purposes and one folding blade for utilitarian purposes, but this is purely personal preference. A good blade is a multi-purpose tool.

Ideally, if you have the means, you'll learn how to use your blade. This includes knife fighting. I recommend martial arts training to every would-be magician. Not only does it teach fighting skills, which are always useful in this day and age, but it helps instill discipline, grounds a person in their own skin, and can teach a thing or two about the flow of energy in the body.

Steel has certain properties and blades are useful in consecrating a space. Power can be drawn up and channeled through the blade. They can also be used to cut etheric cords. This is an important function. Whenever we interact with someone on a physically intimate level (particularly during sex) connections of energy, magic, and intent are formed. These etheric cords ensure that energy is shared between the two people and tie the people together magically and spiritually unless they are consciously cut. If one person is a magician, it is very easy to influence the other through these connections. This is the reason why so many traditional spells call for someone belonging to the intended victim: a picture, nail clippings, hair, semen, blood, or even a piece of clothing. (See Appendix: Three Principal Laws of Magic).

Sometimes when one is under magical attack, it is because someone is using one of these cords (regardless of how the cord was formed) as a link to the victim. In cases like this, it is necessary to cut the etheric cord, which can occasionally be somewhat unpleasant. Anyone with Sight can actually see these cords, but if a person with that particular talent isn't available, it's often possible to use your own intuition to ferret out where the cord is connecting. Usually they connect at the root, sex, or solar plexus chakras.

To cut the cord, first locate it. Then take the blade in your hands, draw energy up and channel it into the blade. Cut the cord (not the person!) just as you would a piece of rope or string. Then seal the person by marking a protective sigil with oil or red ochre over the spot where the cord was cut.

Blades should not be cleansed with salt water. It is best to clean them with sacred smoke. Be sure to oil the blade appropriately after cleansing, wiping off any excess oil before storing it in its sheath.

The Tool of Fire: The Wand

Magically, fire is usually associated with the will, strength, courage, passion, transformation and destruction. The negative traits of this element are lack of control over one's passions, and anger management issues. The traditional direction of this element is South, its colors are vibrant reds and oranges, and its traditional tool is the wand.

When I was training, I was required to make my own wand. I chose the wood very carefully, sanded it down, wood burned the appropriate sigils on it (in my case, runes) affixed a stone at the bottom and a pointed crystal at the tip, binding them with copper wire and adding decorative leather. It was a potent meditation. Admittedly though, I usually use the knife for anything that a more traditional magician would utilize the wand for. If you feel the need to make a wand, know that it represents fire and is used to stir up and direct magical energy. In some ceremonial traditions, the knife is the tool of fire and the wand of air (which makes more sense to me actually, as the wand is used to direct energy) but this is definitely a minority opinion.

The Tool of Water: The Chalice

Magically, water is usually associated with psychism, the emotions, magic, intuition and dreaming. The negative traits of this element are indecisiveness and excessive emotionality. The traditional direction of this element is West, its colors are deep blues and its traditional tool is the chalice.

I've never understood why water is so often dismissed as a weak element. It's anything but. Water is one of the strongest elements out of the four. It's incredibly flexible: it can become steam, remain in liquid form, or transform into ice and yet it maintains its essential nature. It can be every bit as destructive and vicious as fire; just witness the destruction of the tsunami or the hurricane. The attributions that I've given above are the traditional ceremonial magic attributions. Norse cosmology, for example, would assign far different roles to water, for in this world-matrix, the universe was created through a conflagration of ice and fire and it's a toss up as to which was the dominant element. I've occasionally used a mortar and pestle to represent both earth and water, but this is not in any way traditional.

When using the chalice to represent water, it's usually filled with water. I've found this to be surprisingly useful during workings and magically, having the four tools and elements present does remind one of their power and how it can be properly utilized in a working. It's a reminder to be respectful and to seek balance in these things.

Using the chalice (or bowl, there's nothing wrong with using a bowl) to hold whatever infusions you're making to cleanse your home is a good idea. If you use a tool repeatedly for magic, it picks up a magical charge. It becomes empowered and this power can assist in charging whatever it holds. Personally, I think this is the real reason that the use of these tools is so widespread. Magicians tend to be territorial and that extends to investing their tools with a certain amount of power. After I've gone through the trouble, for instance, of consecrating a knife or a bowl, of charging it, why would I want to repeat that? It makes more pragmatic sense just to use the same bowl or knife over and over again.

The Tool of Earth: The Pentacle

Magically, earth is usually associated with healing, fertility, growth, and the ancestors. The negative traits of this element are excessive sensuality and procrastination. The traditional direction of this element is North, its colors are vibrant greens and browns, and its traditional tool is the pentacle, which symbolizes the balanced union of all four classical elements with spirit.

Because the pentacle has become so strongly associated with Wicca, becoming in effect its sacred symbol, I usually prefer to use either a bowl of salt or a crystal or some other type of stone to represent earth when I feel the need to have all four elements represented either in fact or by tool upon my working altar.

The Tool of the Spirit: The Altar

I'm of the opinion that everyone should have an altar. Spiritually, it's a wonderful way to honor the Gods and can be a nice focal point for prayers and offerings. Magically, it gives you a good place to keep your tools and to perform workings that require said tools. It's useful. I prefer to have a waist-high table as my work table. This is separate from my religious altar, because its purpose is completely different. I keep my altar reasonably clean, and I cleanse it magically on a regular basis. This is where I will set up long-term charms. It's where I set my tools to charge. It's where I work any candle magic that I might wish to work. Altars can be in any size, shape, and color. The important thing is that you have a place to work. Anyway, you may never need these tools, but in the event that you do, you have the basic correspondences here.

Casting a Circle

Traditional Wiccan practice uses this before every ritual to consecrate space. Ceremonial magic, from which Wicca originally co-opted the rite, uses it almost as much. I personally don't see the need; when I want to work magic, I sit down and do so. If you feel the need to ward your space, then work in your own permanently warded house. Ritually casting a circle is a nice way to psychologically signify that one is moving out of normal space and into ritual space, but magically its uses are far more restricted.

A magical circle is indeed used to ward space, but it's used to ward a specific and restricted space. I would use a circle if I wanted to contain something, or if I needed to put people or things in a protected space while I worked outside of that space. That's about it, but then I emphasize pragmatism and efficiency. Your mileage may vary here. If you really feel the need to cast a circle every single time you work, go for it. To my mind though, it's a waste of energy better spent elsewhere.

How to Cast a Circle

I am not going to discuss the myriad of ways one can do this in a ritual setting, be that ritual magical or religious. I'm going to focus on the very narrow magical usage described above. There are a couple of ways to cast a circle outside of the dog-and-pony show of a full ceremonial rite (which I'm not going into here, as there are plenty of books that deal with this already).

Personally, I carry chalk in my magical kit and when I need to ward something, if I'm in a place where I can do so, I draw the circle out with chalk. During this, I verbally calling forth power and channel it into this act, saying something along the lines of: "I consecrate this circle of power that it may bind and protect, keeping out all that would do harm. So mote it be." One can sprinkle salt around the object or person one desires to ward. Salt is very protective and purifying by its very nature. One could take one's blade or wand, center, draw power up and channel it through the tool walking in a clockwise circle around the space one wishes to ward also verbally consecrating it.

Those are my three quick fix ways of doing this. When whatever purpose for which I needed the circle is done, the energy should be broken by either tracing over it clockwise with knife or wand, or consciously dispersing it and grounding it into the earth. It is extremely rare that I need any more ritual than that.

Part 2:

Basic Energy Work

Dealing With Energy Work

Magic, simply put, is the craft of utilizing energy directly through the conduit of the will and body to effect circumstances in a clearly defined and predictable manner. It is not the "art of changing consciousness at will" as Dion Fortune says. That describes a useful technique, not magic itself. It is not prayer, as many Neo-Pagans believe. As I've already touched upon, the two things are as completely different as apples and oranges. Magic is about the conscious application of raw power, and anyone who tells you differently doesn't know much about magic.

All of the props and tools mentioned in this and many other books on the subject are tangential to this truism. They are tools to help focus the will, or to make the process easier, but they are not, in and of themselves, necessary. There's the old axiom repeated by many teachers of the Art that one should be able to work magic effectively in the nude, in an empty room at four a.m., and that axiom holds true. To work magic effectively, two things are needed: sensitivity to energy and a disciplined will (although a high tolerance to pain and discomfort doesn't hurt either).

The aforementioned sensitivity is an inborn gift, just like the psi-talents mentioned in chapter three. It enables one to sense or see the energy currents in one's vicinity and to pull them up so that they can be used. How this talent manifests can be very different depending on what other psi-talents one has. While the psi-talents are not magic, they do make the application of magic much, much easier—otherwise, it can be like working blind. There's also the fact that magical work can open otherwise latent gifts.

Most people with strong gifts also have at least a little talent for working magic, enough to do the various exercises given in this book. That facility can be developed, and it requires honing one's concentration and disciplining one's will. In addition to a daily regimen of centering and grounding, there are dozens of ways that one can perform the most mundane tasks with magical intent, inculcating those tasks with the goal of "training". For instance, if you are a person who tends toward procrastination, consciously forbid yourself this tendency. Nip it in the bud, do not allow it to flower. Change your habitual behavior by conscious and repeated application of will. If you are prone to outbursts of temper, consciously rein this in. If you cannot control your own passions, you cannot effectively or safely practice magic. When you next want to bite the head off of the retail clerk that has annoyed you, curb that impulse and instead be icily polite. It won't kill you and such things go a long way toward developing your willpower. It's not enough to have the gift for sensing and working magic. The magician's primary and most essential tool is a strongly disciplined will.

Learn to curb your appetites. For instance, make it a habit to fast one day a week. If you have a medical condition that precludes this, then limit your food intake to a bit of fruit and grain for the day, drinking only water. There is a classical Roman saying that if one cannot fast for a single day out of the week, then one has no right to call oneself an adult. This helps to subordinate the desires to the will. Desire is good, but only when it is not one's master.

This brings up an important point. The majority of negative energy sent your way, up to and including full-blown attack, is probably not being sent by trained magicians. People can send negative energy without even realizing it. Energy will go wherever will, attention, and intent go. If someone is very jealous, really dislikes a person or is very angry, and actively focuses on this with a sudden burst of energy that energy can unconsciously be directed toward a victim. This is the origin of *malocchio*, or the evil eye. Most people don't shield and they also don't realize that their emotions have the power to harm in this way. Emotion, after all, is energy. You will notice in reading this book that I have not included any techniques for either binding an opponent or hexing him/her. This is largely because it takes more than the knowledge one can glean from a book to ferret out whether an attack is intentional or not. It also takes more than book knowledge to learn how to do either one of these things safely and effectively. The techniques given here will disperse pretty much anything other than a well-planned attack by a trained and highly skilled magician (and quite possibly some of that as well). For that, there is no shame in calling in outside help.

Another facet of magic to consider is that it is an embodied experience, for all that it's also metaphysical. Do what you can to keep yourself in good, healthy physical shape. Working magic can really put a strain on the physical body; offset that by exercising, eating healthily, and trying to get enough sleep—all often easier said than done. Studying a martial art for both the physical discipline and the sensitivity to energy that it brings is an excellent idea, as would be the study of T'ai Chi or Ch'i Gong. Meditating for ten or fifteen minutes a day in a comfortable position wherein you systematically go into your body's muscle memory, consciously relaxing each group of muscles starting at the toes and working up to the crown of the head is also a worthy enterprise. Please do not do this lying down. I've found that it almost inevitably results in a nice, sound sleep before one has reached one's ankles!

That being said, there are a few other basic exercises that one can practice to learn to sense magical energy more strongly and to learn to actively manipulate that energy.

Raising Energy

This is the most basic exercise in energy manipulation. In order to do anything with this energy, you have to learn how to tap into it and actually raise it with your will and mental "hands." Begin by centering and grounding strongly. Extend your senses into the earth and feel for a line of energy. When you feel a little jolt, draw the energy into you through your inward-flowing grounding channel, and allow it to flow into your hands. Your hands may tingle, or you may feel a certain warmth. Either use the energy for something or send it back down through your outward flowing grounding channel.

Energy Balls

After you've learned how to draw energy up, the next exercise is learning how to shape it into something. The most common technique given is the creation of energy balls. Draw energy up and into your hands. Feel or see it glowing there. Consciously shape it with your will and mind into a sphere.

Once you've gotten the hang of this, try make the sphere bigger (feed more energy into it and feel/see it expand) or smaller (feel /see it condensing). To make them stronger, feed more energy into them; to weaken them, ground some energy out of them.

Charging Items

Next, once you've confidently mastered the making of energy balls, try charging an item. Take a coin or a stone and charge the hell out of it. This means raising energy and sending it into the object in question. Seal it in by doing two things: first, cleanly sever any connection the energy may have to you. Do this by consciously tying it off into the object and visualizing a clean separation between you and it. Then, draw a sacred symbol of your choice over the object.

Put that stone or coin amongst a couple of other stones or coins and leave it for a few hours. Come back to it and see if you can tell by feel which is the charged object. Basic candle magic (given below) is an excellent means of learning to charge objects. It's also nice in that it's a simple form of magic and one can, when it's properly focused, see immediate results.

Blood

Blood is the most potent substance you will ever work with, and it creates one of the strongest links possible. That rule applies whether you are using it to create a link to a person, or whether you are using your own blood to bind a tool to your hand alone. It is a powerful, powerful substance.

If you choose to use blood in magic (and some allies will require it—the Germanic rune-spirits certainly do on a regular basis), the most potent blood is that drawn by your own hand with conscious intent. Menstrual blood is, for the most part, utterly useless in magic. It is waste blood. It has some uses in hoodoo love charms, and can occasionally be utilized in fertility magic, but beyond that, it's weak. Better not to use blood at all than to use what is, effectively, a second-rate substance. If you don't have the will to draw blood with a tool, then you don't have the will to work the spell.

The easiest and safest way to draw blood is to use a diabetic lancet. These can be purchased in bulk at most pharmacies. Be sure to clean the puncture afterwards. Each lancet should only be used once and should then be disposed of. I keep a plastic bottle that I use as a sharps container where I collect them and then dispose of the container itself when full. Blood is, medically, a dangerous substance. Don't share implements with anyone. Ever.

Keep in mind that using blood in a charm creates a connection that could be used against you should the charm ever fall into the wrong hands. Guard your blood, it goes without saying, as you would guard your life and do not ever, ever, give it to another magician. That actually goes for menstrual blood as well, for while it isn't as potent as consciously drawn blood in a spell, it still comes from you and can create a magical link. In general, be cautious and don't allow any "personal concerns" (blood, sexual fluids, hair, nail clippings, even clothing) to fall into someone else's hands.

Basic Candle Magic

Candle magic is a very good method of learning how to feel and manipulate energy. It is one of the most basic forms of practical magic, as well as one of the easiest. It's very elemental and simple to practice. There are generally three steps: cleansing, charging, and etching.

Cleansing The Candle

Since candles may have been handled by several people and picked up various energies in their travels, it's good to do a quick and simple cleansing before you set it to your own purpose. I suggest smudging the candle with a purifying herb. When I was a novice, I was instructed to verbally dedicate the candle by saying something to the effect of : *I cleanse, bless and purify this creature of wax for the magic at hand. This creature of wax is cleansed and purified, so mote it be.* You can say this if you want, but why waste words? Do the above steps properly and this stupid phrase is unnecessary.

Charging the Candle

All magic is based on will and intent, so keep this in mind as you set about charging the candle to whatever purpose you have chosen. Again, I was originally told to say *Blessed be this creature of power, you are no more creature of wax, but creature of flesh and blood and you know full well why and for whom you live,* or *Blessed be this creature of magic; this creature of magic is fully alive, alive with purpose; this creature of magic knows well why and for whom it burns.* If you feel the need, go ahead, but I find holding the purpose in my mind and filling the candle with energy works even better.

Ground yourself, feeling your connection to the earth as strongly as possible. Draw energy up and feel it flowing through your body, into your hands and into the candle. Try to avoid using your internal energies – the power source is very limited. Once you master this drawing up and focusing of energy into the candle itself, it may actually shake in your hands, your hands may get hot, the candle may melt a bit or it may feel heavier – in other words, you may notice something. Continue sending energy into it, all the while setting that energy to the purpose you have chosen. This is done by focusing intently on what you want and feeling the energy take on the shape and texture of that desire, imprinting the energy with that desire. Once you feel you have enough energy in the candle, seal it in by making (with fingers or knife) an invoking pentacle on it. Start at the point, move to lower left corner, up to upper right, across to upper left corner, down to lower right, up to point and make a clockwise circle.

At this point, you may want to carve onto the candle certain sigils, runes, etc to add more power. Keep the intent fully in mind as you carve. You can use a knife, pin, whatever works best. Runes respond very well to being fed a bit of blood. If you choose to feed the runes this way, use a diabetic lancet to draw the blood, discarding it after use. Put a few drops on the rune.

If you're using a seven-day candle, the kind that pulls out of the glass, and you want to get extra fancy, here are some traditional things you can add at this point:

1. Iron filings in the bottom of the glass to draw down energy.
2. Honey. This is good in love and prosperity spells because it honors the Goddess Ochun who rules those things. Be sure to taste the honey first before putting it in the glass. This is Ochun's favorite food, but it is traditional to taste it first because in one story someone tried to poison Ochun by giving her poisoned honey.
3. Dragon's blood powder, which is especially good for protections or combat magic. Any incense or finely ground herb can be used in this manner.
4. Pennies to represent wealth and manifestation.
5. Oils of choice. Use ones that match the purpose of the magic.

Be creative here, if you choose to do this. Some people even light a spoonful of incense and dump that in the bottom of the jar then cover it so the jar fills with smoke. I usually don't bother with any of this.

Once you've charged and carved the candle, take an oil of your choice that matches the purpose of the casting, pour some into your hand, and rub it all over the candle. More words to say (if you choose) are; *With this oil and by and through these hands, I now empower this creature of magic to bring forth and manifest that which I desire, that which I will.*

As you rub the oil into the candle, keep your intent in mind. This is also a good time to also add more energy. Unless the candle ignites in your hand, you have not added too much energy.

Pick a resin or ground herb or powder—I usually use dragon's blood—and rub it into the carving (which may be somewhat melted from the heat of your hands, but that's OK). This will highlight the carving. I use dragon's blood because it augments almost any magic and can draw powerful energy. It does make a mess, though, and doesn't wash off your hands very well.

If you really want to say more words you might try: *This spell cannot be changed or altered by anyone or anything in any way or any manner. As is my will, so mote it be.* This seals the charm. At this point, make another invoking pentacle, and clap your hands to shake off any excess energy. Make sure there are no cords linking you to the magic. Try to see all ties breaking as you clap your hands. Then light the candle with intent. It's best to leave it burning, but if this isn't possible, it's fine to blow it out so long as you re-light with as much intent as the first time.

When you are working any type of magic, have one and only one, clear purpose in mind. Working magic is rather like giving instructions to a four-year-old. Keep it simple. The size of the candle doesn't matter at all. It's the intent with which it is used, empowered and lit. It's all about will. In other words, it's all in how you use it.

Candles that cannot be removed from the jar can be empowered in the same way as above, just do the carving and oiling on the very top and use a marker to draw whatever sigils you wish on the glass. It's always good to carve or write the name and astrological sign of the person for whom the spell is being done on the candle.

Types of Candles

Skull Candles: White: uncrossings, healings, bringing clarity. Black: absorbs negativity. Red: love spells, or to really get inside someone's head.

Man/woman figure candles: This is sympathetic magic, good for love and healings.

Cat candles: Uncrossings.

Cross candles: Psychic work, protections, uncrossings.

Seven Knobbed Candles: Burn one knob a day while focusing intently on one's purpose. Choose by color of candle.

Penis/Vagina Candles: Sex magic, fertility, love, lust, also to represent Gods and Goddesses.

Witch candles: Good luck

Seven African Powers: Prayer, devotion and uncrossings.

An uncrossing is a hoodoo term for a spell performed to cleanse one of all negativity, or to break a hex that has been cast upon you. In this parlance, to cross someone is to lay a spell on them, to uncross is to break such a spell. When in doubt as to a color, choose white. Eventually it doesn't really matter, if one's intent is strong. The colors simply help the caster focus his or her intent. If you have preconceived negative feelings about a certain color, it's probably best not to use it. Any candle may be used for devotional purposes; charge it with energy as a gift, or simply light it.

Colors

Black: Absorbs energy; it's the absence of color. It can be used in retribution type spells. It may also be used in certain uncrossings and warfetters (bindings). Its planetary correspondence is Saturn.

Brown: Grounding, earth work. Its planetary correspondence is Earth, though I prefer to use this color for Saturn.

Purple: Psychic development, crown chakra work, expansion, wealth, wisdom. Its planetary correspondence is Jupiter.

Blue: Calming, protection, peace, blessings, healing. Relates to water, fertility, psychic matters. Its planetary correspondence is Neptune and the moon.

Green: Money, earth, fertility, abundance, harvest, healing, removing stress. Its planetary correspondence is the Earth.

Yellow: Healing, especially respiratory distress; can evoke the sun via a solar blast of energy, energy work, inspiration, creativity, success, fame, etc. Its planetary correspondence is the Sun.

Orange: Success, opens stuff up, uncrossings, clarity, knowledge, intellectual endeavors. Its planetary correspondence is Mercury.

Red: Force of will, energy, courage, battle, valor, intensity, lust, passion. Its planetary correspondence is Mars.

Pink: Love, romance, friendship, relationships, happiness. Its planetary correspondence is Venus.

Gold: Can be solar, healing, success. Its planetary correspondence is the Sun.

Silver: Psychic development, dream work, uncrossings. Its planetary correspondence is the moon.

Grey: Neutralizes bad situations, uncrossings, addiction breaking, banishings. It's good to burn these now and again to cleanse. These are very good for bindings as well.

White: When in doubt use white. It is good for all magic, healings, pretty much anything. Its planetary correspondence is moon.

Traditionally, the time of the waxing moon is good for manifesting things, the waning moon for removing negative influences, the full moon for all positive workings and the dark moon for hexing, warfetters, etc. Just as stones and herbs have specific energy resonances, so do colors and moon phases. Some people are more sensitive to this than others and like to include these things in their work.

Wyrd

As a last note, I want to say something about the proper attitude of a magician when attempting to affect the universe.

The way that I practice magic is, as I noted earlier, largely informed by my religious practices and the cosmology in which I work, which is Norse. Within Norse cosmology, an inherent part of the structure of the universe is a concept called *wyrd*. This concept is often linked with Fate, but most people have a very limited and static idea of what Fate is, and *wyrd* is much more than some destiny set in stone. *Wyrd* is causality and consequence. It's partially inherited luck and obligation, but at the same time it is also comprised of our own actions, choices, successes and failures. We can shape our *wyrd* to some degree, making it stronger or weaker by the choices we make and how we behave. *Wyrd* is so powerful that even the Gods must obey it. This force is usually seen as a vast, complex web stretching further than the eye can see. It's like a layered maze of ley lines that can be felt, read, and sometimes actively manipulated. Every single person has their own personal thread of *wyrd*, called *orlog*.

Because *wyrd* connects all living things, because it forms the fabric out of which the world is made, it's possible to navigate it. Reading the threads of *wyrd* and what they contain is a psychic art that the ancient Norse called *spae*. Working it directly, altering its flow, reweaving the threads, is a powerful and dangerous kind of magic, not to be undertaken without a full understanding of the situation and, ideally, permission from the Norns (the three Fates who guard the web of *Wyrd*). Attempting to influence causality itself is not a safe or easy thing. When you do magic and it doesn't work, it might be that there wasn't enough power, it might be that your aim was off ... or it might be that your spell struck the web of *Wyrd* and bounced off, that the Universe determined that this was just not meant to be.

It is through careful examination of the threads that one can determine what magic can lawfully be cast, and how best to cast for good effect. It is also possible to read the consequences of what one is casting, and possible repercussions. *Wyrd* is created by the sum total of our actions and choices, combined with those of our ancestors which we inherit. It is a powerful force in and of itself and should not be underestimated or treated disrespectfully. This is why it's useful for magic-workers to learn some form of divination (or be good friends with some diviners) so as to check on the wisdom and efficacy of any spell that they might cast.

Remember that all your actions stay in the thread of your *wyrd*, and must be worked out through your *orlog*. There is no getting away from this, no magic that you can do to bypass responsibility for your actions. Remember this every time that you do a magical working, and think about how it will affect the greater Web.

Part 3:

Appendices

Appendix I: Symptoms of Magical/Psychic Attack

(Many of these symptoms are physical. Before assuming there's been an attack, please make sure that all is right with your physical health. See your doctor to rule out health issues. In the case of true attack, there will always be at least three of these symptoms present.)

1. Unexpected and negative occurrences in your vicinity and the vicinity of your loved ones and friends.

2. Unexplained "bad" luck, more than can be explained by mere coincidence, in every aspect of your life: relationships, work, finances, health.

3. Close calls that could easily have resulted in fatality. For example, I know one magician who was fighting off a very strong attack. One day the attack manifested in a traffic light crashing down onto his car. Had he not been properly warded, and very, very skilled at shielding, he'd have been killed.

4. Exhaustion.

5. Headaches.

6. Lack of energy or motivation.

7. Nightmares.

8. An unexplained feeling of being stalked, hunted or watched.

9. General ill health coinciding with at least two of the other symptoms listed here.

10. Conflict in relationships for no apparent reason: both professional and personal relationships. This often occurs out of the blue and escalates.

11. Depression and nervous anxiety.

12. Electrical problems.

13. Things breaking in your general vicinity, particularly electronic equipment. (This can also happen with strongly gifted people who are emotionally upset and not shielding properly.)

14. Unusual and unpleasant smells in your home or working space for no logical reason.

First Steps to Take in Case of Psychic or Magical Attack

1.   First, if you have a suspicion about who is attacking you, return, burn or discard any item that you have received from that person.

2.   Take a cleansing bath, and then clean your house thoroughly, first physically and then magically.

3.   Go over all your wards and personal shields. Make sure they are in top working order.

4.   If you know who is attacking you, or have a strong suspicion, avoid all contact with this person and for Gods' sake, don't accept any gifts, food, or drink from that person.

5.   Go over your aura and make sure there are no holes or tears. Cleanse regularly.

6.   If possible, take a vacation. Get away from your regular environment. This can help break the link your enemy has on you.

7.   If you are religious, make offerings to your Gods and engage in a regular daily prayer practice. This has a surprising amount of power.

8.   Make offerings to your ancestors and any other allies you may have. Explain what is happening and ask for their direct and active protection.

9.   Perform whatever uncrossings or banishing rituals you have in your arsenal.

10.   Schedule an appointment with a good diviner. Have a full reading on the situation. It doesn't hurt to get a second opinion and to call in backup. A specialist may be able to point out something that you've missed. Obviously, it goes without saying, don't go to a storefront psychic. Ideally, seek out an experienced spirit-worker, magician or shaman.

Appendix 2: Three Principal Laws of Magic

While there are more laws than this in the magical world, the following three are, to my mind, the most important.

1. The Law of Sympathy

This law states that "like attracts like". This means that certain objects sharing specific characteristics can be used to symbolize greater objects that reflect the same characteristics: thus, gold is symbolic of the power of the sun, silver of the moon. You can also use the lesser object in place of the greater, and the greater will respond in a similar manner to the way in which you treat the lesser. For example, you create a poppet of a person utilizing a picture of them or a clipping of hair, and what is done to the poppet will affect the person that it represents. This leads us directly to law number two:

2. The Law of Contagion

This law states that what was once part of you always remains part of you. An action taken on the part will then similarly affect the whole. This law also states that when two disparate things are in physical contact, an etheric or astral bond is created. This is particularly important in sexual intercourse. Keep in mind that through the exchange of energy and/or body fluids, a powerful magical connection is being created. This is also the reason so many spells call for "personal concerns": fingernail clippings, a piece of hair, body fluids. It gives a powerful line right under a person's shields, because what was once a part of a person remains tied to them. Even photos can hold a certain amount of energy.

3. The Law of Negative Rebound

This law is of utmost importance in combat, attack and by extension protection. This law states that if the object of an attack is too well shielded for the attack to find its mark, it will hit the weakest point closest to the target. For instance: someone throws a magical attack at you and instead of hitting you, it hits your cat, which dies. Or instead of hitting you physically, it hits a weakness in your *wyrd* and you lose your job, or your car takes the attack for you and dies. Sometimes, if you are wearing magically protective jewelry, the jewelry can suddenly break, having absorbed the attack.

The corollary to this is that if you throw an attack and your opponent is too well-shielded and has taken precautions to make sure that all weak spots are shielded, or actively deflects the attack back, you as the caster can get hit, either with backlash from the reflected spell or with negative rebound on yourself!

Note: there is no such thing as the "law of three". The whole Wiccan idea of the "threefold return" has no basis in magical fact.

Appendix 3: Sigils and Runes

Symbols mentioned in the text:

Uncrossing

Helm of Awe

Pentacle

The Rune Chart on the following page lists the 24 Norse Futhark runes and the additional 9 Anglo-Saxon runes. The Norse names come first, and the names in parentheses are Anglo-Saxon. An abbreviated keyword meaning for each rune is in bold beneath the names. These are complex symbols with many layers of meanings which are beyond the scope of this book. You can use the keywords given with each rune for creating magical charms, but if you want to use runes as a regular part of your practice, you should bother to learn about the system in more depth in order to have a better understanding of what you are working with.

Many of the books on Norse cosmology and magic listed in the resources section have additional in-depth information on runes.

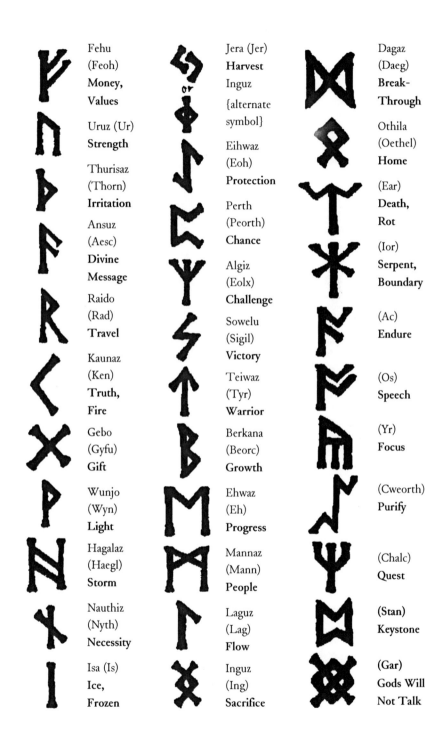

Fehu
(Feoh)
Money,
Values

Uruz (Ur)
Strength

Thurisaz
(Thorn)
Irritation

Ansuz
(Aesc)
Divine
Message

Raido
(Rad)
Travel

Kaunaz
(Ken)
Truth,
Fire

Gebo
(Gyfu)
Gift

Wunjo
(Wyn)
Light

Hagalaz
(Haegl)
Storm

Nauthiz
(Nyth)
Necessity

Isa (Is)
Ice,
Frozen

Jera (Jer)
Harvest

Inguz
{alternate
symbol}

Eihwaz
(Eoh)
Protection

Perth
(Peorth)
Chance

Algiz
(Eolx)
Challenge

Sowelu
(Sigil)
Victory

Teiwaz
(Tyr)
Warrior

Berkana
(Beorc)
Growth

Ehwaz
(Eh)
Progress

Mannaz
(Mann)
People

Laguz
(Lag)
Flow

Inguz
(Ing)
Sacrifice

Dagaz
(Daeg)
Break-
Through

Othila
(Oethel)
Home

(Ear)
Death,
Rot

(Ior)
Serpent,
Boundary

(Ac)
Endure

(Os)
Speech

(Yr)
Focus

(Cweorth)
Purify

(Chalc)
Quest

(Stan)
Keystone

(Gar)
Gods Will
Not Talk

Appendix 4: Suggested Resources

Bauschatz, Paul, (1982). *The Well and the Tree*. MA: University of Massachusetts Press.

Coleman, Martin, (1998). *Communing with Spirits*. ME: Samuel Weiser, Inc.

Cunningham, Scott, (1996). *Crystal, Gem & Metal Magic*. MN: Llewellyn Publications, Inc.

Denning, Melita & Phillips, Osborne, (2002). *Practical Guide to Psychic Self-Defense*. MN: Llewellyn Publications.

Fortune, Dion, (2000). *Esoteric Orders and Their Work*. ME: Samuel Weiser, Inc.

Fortune, Dion, (1997). *Psychic Self Defense*. ME: Samuel Weiser, Inc.

Fortune, Dion, (2000). *The Training and Work of an Initiate*. ME: Samuel Weiser, Inc.

Hope, Murry, (2001). *The World of Psychism*. UK: Thoth Publications.

Kaldera, Raven & Schwartzstein, Tannin, (2002). *The Urban Primitive*. MN: Llewellyn Publications, Inc.

Kaldera, Raven, (2007). *Pathwalker's Guide to the Nine Worlds*. MA: Asphodel Press.

Kaldera, Raven, (2007). *Wightridden: Techniques of Northern Tradition Shamanism*. MA: Asphodel Press.

Kaldera, Raven, (2007). *Wyrdwalkers: Techniques of Northern Tradition Shamanism*. MA: Asphodel Press.

King, Francis & Skinner, Stephen, (2000). *Techniques of High Magic*. VT: Destiny Books.

Krasskova, Galina, (2005). *Exploring the Northern Tradition*. NJ: New Page Books.

Mauss, Marcel, (2006). *A General Theory of Magic*. UK: Routledge.

Mickaharic, Draja, (1995). *Practice of Magic*. ME: Samuel Weiser, Inc.

Mickaharic, Draja, (2002). *Spiritual Worker's Spellbook*. ME: Samuel Weiser, Inc.

Mickaharic, Draja, (2002). *Magical Techniques*. US: Xlibris.

Mickaharic, Draja, (2002). *Mental Influence*. US: Xlibris.

Nema, (2003). *The Way of Mystery*. MN: Llewellyn Publications, Inc.

Paxson, Diana, (2006). *Essential Asatru*. NY: Citadel Press.

Regardie, Israel, (1981). *The One Year Manual: Twelve Steps to Spiritual Enlightenment*. ME: Samuel Weiser, Inc.

Yronwode, Catherine, (2002). *Hoodoo Herb and Root Magic*. CA: Lucky Mojo publishing. (I also highly recommend her hoodoo and rootwork course offered at www.luckymojo.com.)

About the Author

Sophie Reicher has been a practicing occultist for twenty years. She currently lives in New York where she is working on her second book.

Breinigsville, PA USA
09 June 2010
239575BV00001B/67/P